T0323500

Building Businesses from the Inside Out

As businesses grow, culture can be created by accident or by design. This book is for coaches and consultants who want to support their clients to design their culture.

Coaches can struggle to devise simple and useful content, especially if they are new to coaching. This book gives clear models and frameworks as well as the steps to deliver those frameworks to their clients. Based on the popular Kick A** Culture Coach Program, it is full of new ideas, tried and tested models, and thoughts on how to develop a deeper relationship with clients through retained programs. Unique to this book are the links provided to online courses, with each chapter including a link to an online course which helps to embed learning and gives access to downloadable materials, such as video, audio, and high quality, professionally designed PDFs suitable for workshops, presentations, and coaching sessions.

This book is a comprehensive resource for experienced business coaches and consultants to add to their toolkits, as well as aspiring coaches and consultants who need frameworks to get started – and it's helpful for business owners too.

Rebecca Bonnington was born in Banbury, but raised in Manchester from the age of one. Her down-to-earth, no-nonsense approach to business coaching and consulting has served her clients well over the past 15 years. She lives in Edinburgh with her husband, youngest daughter, and two dogs. Her two older children live close by. She's the CEO and co-founder of Tricres and describes herself as the business coach's coach.

Building Businesses from the Inside Out

A Coach's Guide to Developing Awesome Cultures in Business

Rebecca Bonnington

Routledge
Taylor & Francis Group

NEW YORK AND LONDON

Designed cover image: Lauren Jones

First published 2025
by Routledge
605 Third Avenue, New York, NY 10158

and by Routledge
4 Park Square, Milton Park, Abingdon, Oxon, OX14 4RN

Routledge is an imprint of the Taylor & Francis Group, an informa business

ISBN: 9781032889917 (hbk)
ISBN: 9781032882208 (pbk)
ISBN: 9781003540694 (ebk)

DOI: 10.4324/9781003540694

Typeset in Sabon
by codeMantra

Contents

Why Have I Written This Book and Who Is It For?

The wonderful people who learn and qualify with us as Kick A** Culture Coaches and Consultants asked us to write this book.

#

We've created a fabulous online learning platform for you. Many of you also wanted a book to go with the videos and PDFs we've got online.

#

Each chapter of this book highlights an individual course and outlines the details of its origin story, who the model or framework was created for, and why it was created.

#

Then we show you how to use the model or framework, when to use it, and what questions to ask your clients to find out if they need it. We also give you the questions to ask whilst you're using the model or framework.

#

In the best tradition of coaching and consulting, we give you a case study and a real-life example of how the content was used with some additional notes or completed matrices if that's appropriate.

#

At its heart, this is a Tricres book so it's true to our values; direct, bold, and impactful. No nonsense, just straightforward, clear, and concise, using words that are easy to follow.

#

If you're a coach, consultant, or client and want to get into the nitty gritty of our Kick A** Culture Coach and Consultant Program, then this book is most definitely for you. Whilst you can read it and use its content to inform your own business without doing our online program, you'll get much more from it if you use it alongside our online program.

#

Enjoy.

How Should You Use This Book?

Each chapter focuses on a model or framework. Each model or framework is designed to tackle something specific within a growing business.

#

At Tricres, we think about businesses as a human being. It has a personality, as well as needs, wants, and desires. To make life easy, we break businesses down into three key areas:

#

1 People
2 Strategy
3 Revenues

#

All of these are wrapped up and supported by the culture of the business.

#

The three areas of a business overlap. Nothing works in a straight line (sorry), so we've laid out the chapters roughly in the order in which you might use them with a client. However (and it's a big HOWEVER), each client is different so you may well start with a different model and there are some models you may never use with a client because it's just not appropriate.

#

Each chapter heading looks like this:

#

Chapter 1
PEOPLE: Culture as a Foundation for Growth

#

So you'll know which part of the business this model falls into.

#

You can read this book in any order you wish. Use it as a refresher before seeing a client or even take it with you. Clients are also able to purchase the book if they wish, they'll still need you to coach and consult with them so don't panic, you won't be replaced by a book or online course.

Chapter 1

Culture as a Foundation for Growth in Businesses

The People category features other models such as:

- Employee Engagement
  - Talent Acquisition and Retention, Succession Planning
  - Performance Management
  - Constructive Conversations
  - Great Team Development

Each of these has their own chapter.

As I worked with more and more leaders, I realized that it wasn't just the systems and processes in their businesses that needed work. I'd often help the leaders to change their thinking or behaviors to get better results and then look at the rest of the business and realize it was pretty dysfunctional.

This often led the person I was coaching to leave the business. A great result for them, but the business lost a brilliant person who could have really made a difference.

It became obvious that the leader, the CEO, Founder, or Managing Partner of the business set the tone for the culture. I watched Simon Sinek's famous TEDTalk "How Leaders Inspire Action" and realized what I was talking about was the 'why' or, as I like to call it, the "purpose" of the business.

Once you discover the purpose of a business beyond profit, I knew I could unpack the vision and then the values. By this time, a friend of mine had introduced me to a system he used. This framework helped me understand that adding systems to the end of the framework helped businesses embed their culture rather than sit around staring at lovely pictures of words on a wall.

Here's the framework I adapted from my friend Jim. By the way, Jim was a very senior Head of Learning and Development for a huge organization in the NHS here in the UK, so he knew what he was talking about.

DOI: 10.4324/9781003540694-1

Values Grid

VALUE	MEANING	BEHAVIOUR	SUPPORTING SYSTEM
Bold	• • •	• • •	
Impactful	• • •	• • •	
Direct	• • •	• • •	

Figure 1.1 Values Grid, Blank Version.

I did further research on how culture impacts the performance of a business and discovered it has rather beneficial effects. Not only can a clear, positive culture add up to 60% more value to a business, it also creates happier places to work.

Fewer people leave, better people apply (when I say 'better' I mean people who are ideally suited to that particular business), fewer people are off sick, and the succession plan is easier to fulfil as people stay longer and tend to be more productive.

The capitalist hippy in me thought this was a brilliant balance of hard-nosed commerciality and lovely places to work.

So, Culture as a Foundation for Growth was born. I designed, with the ever-patient Lauren Jones (our Head of Brand and Founder of Brand by Boudica), a series of circles to illustrate this and realized my method was about building businesses from the inside out.

As Simon Sinek said, most people start from the outside in. They build systems that create toxic cultures, not on purpose, but that tends to be the outcome. The systems are built for spreadsheets and reporting and not for people. The trick is to combine both. Systems that first work for people and then work for the accountants.

Let's start with the conversation you're having with a potential client. I would always start these first chats over coffee or Zoom with the simple question, 'tell me about your business.'

Usually twenty to thirty minutes later I had the whole story, warts and all. It's really important when your prospective client is talking to you about their business that you sit quietly and listen. I ask occasional questions for clarity, but otherwise I listen.

You can find out how I conduct these meetings by reading the chapter on Constructive Conversations. I even give you lists of questions to ask.

Your clients or prospects will be asking you these kinds of questions, which is how you know culture or lack of vision, direction is an issue.

- How do I attract and retain the best talent for my business, particularly in a competitive market?
- How do I make really good, fast strategic decisions and how do I know they're good decisions for my business?
- How do I create stronger, longer-lasting client and customer relationships for my business (this includes online and offline)?
- I'd like to leave a great legacy and a sustainable business, how do I do that beyond the balance sheet?
- How do I maximize the value of my business without having to increase revenues or profits?

They're highlighted in bullet point because these feature in the 'motherboard' PDF that accompanies Culture as a Foundation for Growth. I get copies of this PDF printed for my clients when I'm delivering the Purpose, Vision, and Values Day. I'd encourage you to do the same, see the end of the chapter for the QR Code to access materials.

In the same PDF, I also highlight how the model is useful, which is what I say to clients when I'm talking to them about it, here's what I say....

TOP TIP, I don't 'tell, I ask. So I turn these statements into questions.

- Your business is stuck and you can't understand why you're not attracting or retaining great people
- You have a very high staff turnover
- Everything else is working well, but you feel something is missing
- You want to expand, open more offices, merge or acquire other businesses and need it to succeed quickly
- You're looking to sell your business
- You want to create leaders of the future and a strong succession

Even though this model is the first one I tend to use with clients to deliver work, the one-day session I use to deliver it is called a Purpose, Vision, and Values Day. I called it that because clients don't necessarily understand Culture as a Foundation for Growth Day.

A business that can't make clear, conscious choices, or that can't attract the right people, hold onto the right people, or decide where it's heading is a business that's going to eventually fail. It's certainly going to struggle to be as profitable or as successful as it might be with great decision-making, the right people, and knowing exactly where it's heading.

Business owners get this and are usually very happy to invest a day's worth of time and money to sort this out. Business owners who don't get this aren't the right clients for you, so move on.

I charge my full-day rate for this and insist all the stakeholders are there on the day. Because this is the first piece of work I deliver after the Fact Find, I've already met those stakeholders, built rapport, and got to know the business, so this next step is fairly easy to book in the diary.

I'll get to the Fact Find bit at the end of the book. We need to go through each model first.

Ok, so you need to know how to deliver the Purpose, Vision, and Values workshop. I've given you the agenda here.

ABC Company
Purpose, Vision, and Values Day

Venue: London
Date: 12th October 2024
Time: 09:30 to 16:30

Proposed Agenda
09:30   Welcome and scene setting
10:00   Introductions, Rebecca to the Partners and the Partners to Rebecca
10:15   Context – Re-energize
        Culture, introduction, and why it's important
        What you want from today
        A short video, Simon Sinek's TEDTalk on "How Great Leaders Inspire Action"
11:00   Coffee break
11:15   Purpose (what are we here for?) – use the questions in the "finding your purpose" document"
12:00   Vision (big big picture), ten years from now, where do you want to be?
        Focus on big, hairy audacious vision. It's about imagining where you want to be.
12:30   Values exercise (mixing things up). Ask the following four questions:

        1   What are we brilliant at?
        2   What's the best thing about working here?
        3   What would our competitors be envious of?
        4   Describe our character and personality
            Place sticky notes under the question headings around the room.
            Collate the themes from each heading and write them up on a board. The common words and themes are the values of the business. You need three.

13:00 Lunch
13:45 Thinking creatively on purpose – this exercise is found in Thinking
       Big Part 4
14:30 PATH, this exercise is found in Thinking Big Part 4
15:00 Coffee
15:15 PATH continued
16:00 Round up, next steps
16:15 Key Learnings
16:30 Close

There's more information on our learning platform with videos and audio to help you. See the QR Code at the end of this chapter for more information.

You'll need to review Culture as a Foundation for Growth ground-level course.

You'll need to review Part 4 of Thinking Big (really big) for the Thinking Creatively On Purpose Exercise.

You'll need to review Part 4 of Thinking Big (really big) for the PATH exercise.

All of these details are in this book and even more detail and information is available online.

Outcomes

On every client interaction I have, I make sure there are clear outcomes. I document these in an Update Note document. I'll cover that soon. For now, we need to stick with the culture piece.

The outcomes from the one-day Purpose, Vision, and Values workshop are best illustrated with our simple grid, it looks like this (see the next page for the grid). This is the Values Grid for Tricres. You client's values grid will have different words in it, but the pattern will be the same.

There are always three values because no one can remember more than that. There are meanings attached to the values so everyone knows what they're talking about. Each value has a set of behaviors attached to it. These will be used later in the Talent Acquisition and Pipeline course. The behaviors are embedded into the supporting systems of the business.

When I work with clients, we produce this grid and then I set to work with their head of sales, marketing, HR and operations to make sure each of the systems within those functions have the behaviors embedded.

For example, HR will more than likely need to change the appraisal and performance management systems in the business to reflect the correct behaviors. Sales will more than likely need to change their targets to ensure they're aligned with the behaviors they want to see in the business.

All promotions in the business will now be based on behaviors and commercial targets. It's only by embedding the values in this way that a business can change and really embrace a positive culture.

Boards must understand that decisions will now be based on values. This may mean turning out seemingly lucrative commercial opportunities, however, if they're not aligned with their values, such opportunities are likely to fail anyway or at least become unprofitable over the long term.

Values Grid

VALUE	MEANING	BEHAVIOUR	SUPPORTING SYSTEM
Bold	• Brave • Fearless • Challenging	• We stand by what we say • We say it as it is • We are leaders	• Our branding and marketing • Our growth plans • International expansion
Impactful	• Disruptive • Inspiring • Empowering	• We challenge the status quo • We instill belief • We make it happen, quicker	• Our learning platform • Our coaching, consulting and training methodology • Our lack of bureaucracy
Direct	• Agile • Creative • Game-changing	• We are flexible • We think outside the box • We deliver WOW results	• Each partner learns a new skill every year • We welcome feedback in all of its forms • We are avid readers, consumers of relevant expertise in all its formats

Figure 1.2 **Example of a Completed Values Grid.**

Follow Up

Sometimes clients will only want one day to re-set their values or identify them. Don't take this personally. You've done a good job and if the business feels it has the in-house expertise and enthusiasm to embed this culture, then leave them to it. I will follow up for the first couple of quarters and then a year later to see how things are going, but otherwise leave them to it.

Then there are businesses who really want your help to get these systems changed. In those instances, I schedule meetings and calls with the relevant heads of function.

Sometimes it's crystal clear who is accountable and responsible for which function and I go ahead and meet them to support them on this journey. Sometimes, it's not at all clear and that's where the next piece of work comes in.

Now is a good time to take a break before we head to Players on the Pitch.

Example of This Working

A small US law firm was able to attract a highly paid lawyer because of their stated culture. They offered the lawyer the job and this person was offered a job at a much higher salary by a much bigger, flashier law firm. He turned the flashier firm's offer down and favor of the smaller law firm. He stated it was the culture that had attracted him.

A medium-sized UK architects firm further enhanced a great culture on the back of this work. During a time when architectural professionals were in high demand and hard to recruit, they had people sending their CVs to them and actively wanting to work with them.

This stuff works.

Figure 1.3 Culture as a Foundation of Growth QR Code.

Chapter 2

Players on the Pitch

Getting the Right People in the Right Roles Doing the Right Jobs

The Strategy category features other models including:

– The Horizon Model
  – Habits and Housekeeping
  – Strategic Thinking Made Easy
  – OKRs Made Easy
  – Growth Accelerator

Each of these has its own chapter.

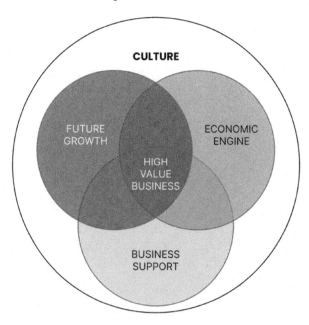

Figure 2.1 Players on the Pitch Circles.

DOI: 10.4324/9781003540694-2

When you have the right people in the right roles doing the right things, the business tends to do better than when people have no idea who is responsible or accountable for what.

Having run many businesses over the years and made every mistake there is to make, I realized that there were a few things I did get right.

Firstly, I made sure I had someone who was completely accountable and responsible for the financial reporting, tax, and bookkeeping part of my business. This is mainly because I once tried to do a VAT (sales tax) return and it took me two days and I still got it wrong. I realized very quickly someone much better than me could do it in a quarter of the time and get it right the first time!

This is the principle of Players on the Pitch. You need to play to people's strengths. Do not expect people to twist themselves into jobs they're not suited to. I've seen owners and leaders try to do that and it simply ends in tears.

If you are a brilliant salesperson, keep selling and recruit other people to do the other stuff in your business. If you're a brilliant IT, ops, or engineering professional, then keep doing that and get a professional CEO in to run the business.

Most professional services businesses, such as law firms, accountants, and architects, fail to do this, which is why many of them end up being swallowed up by the competition or going out of business.

This is how the model came about. I needed my clients to sort out who would be responsible for what so that I knew who to speak to about strategy, people, and revenues.

As with all our core models, your clients will be telling you things that lead you to think about a Players on the Pitch project. Let's look at what your clients might be saying when getting the right people in the right roles doing the right things is an issue for them:

- I have to do everything round here
- No one else can do these things as well as me
- I spend all my time fixing things and have no time to work on the business
- If only everyone was like me
- I can't find the right people to do these things I want to delegate
- It's gone wrong in the past so I don't want to risk delegating things again
- I am overwhelmed and exhausted because of the hours I'm working
- I can't trust people to do it right
- "Do I have to do EVERYTHING ROUND HERE!"
- Remember, each of these statements can be a question too. As a coach and consultant, you can ask these questions which lead to uncovering the client's core issues.

You can use the following ideas to create questions for your potential or existing clients to delve deeper into this issue:

TOP TIP, I don't 'tell,' I ask. You might start your question with 'would you like to have ...'

1 More time to focus on the things you enjoy doing
2 More time to work strategically to grow your business
3 Time away from the business for yourself and your family and friends
4 An increase in engagement from your teams as they feel more empowered (TOP TIP, combining this with the Culture as the Foundation for Growth will support this further)
5 A business that is easier to sell as it no longer relies entirely on you, the owner(s)
6 A more valuable business when you take the Growth Accelerator program, you'll notice that a strong SMT is on the first rung of the scalability ladder
7 Regain your sanity, energy, and enthusiasm for your business

Players on the Pitch is one of the easiest models to convey to your client and can get you some quick wins. It's also the model that you'll need to review regularly as your client's business changes and grows. Finally, it can be one of the hardest to implement if you have an owner, founder, or leader who is reluctant to let go of control.

There's more information on our learning platform with videos and audio to help you. As always, the QR Code is at the end of this chapter.

I also use the very high-level version of this model when I'm doing free talks. I ask the participants to complete a quick review of what they do in a typical week.

They give themselves a percentage score of whether they were focusing on:

1 Business Today – This is what we call the Economic Engine and where a business makes money this year. It includes sales, marketing, operations
2 Future Business – This is the strategic part, where businesses plan where they're going to make the revenues in the next two years
3 Back Office – This is the admin, finance, legal stuff that needs to be done in every business

A rough rule of thumb is that a business owner, leader, or founder should be spending around 60–70% of their time in the Economic Engine, around 10% of their time in Future Growth, and the rest in the Back Office. There is an issue if they're spending all of their time on Back-Office functions or Future Growth because generating revenues for today is being neglected.

I also use this during introductory coffee meetings as it's a quick illustration of where I can bring value.

Outcomes

On each and every client interaction I have, I make sure there are clear outcomes. I document these in an Update Note document. I've attached one at the end of this chapter.

Outcomes from delivering Players on the Pitch can be as simple as a quick realignment of accountabilities and roles if it's a small business or as complex as a complete reorganization.

Much depends on the size of your client's business, who is prepared to delegate what and whether there are people capable of taking on accountability and responsibility for things.

Some recruitment may need to be done.

Job descriptions and an organization chart will certainly need to be produced.

Leadership development training may well be needed. This is the thing I find most often, which is why I designed the 21st Century Leadership Program. The boards of directors I work with often realize they need a strong senior management team (SMT) to take on the accountabilities and responsibilities they have to delegate to grow the business.

Most of the time, the businesses I work with have never invested in leadership development either for themselves or their teams. More of that later though …

Here's an example of an Update Note I send to clients after each interaction.

Update Note
Meeting: Frank and Rebecca
Venue: Cafe MoMo
Date: 3 October 2023
Time: 12:45

Background

Frank is researching potential coaches, trainers, and consultants to work with the senior team at ABC Company.

ABC Company is a business owned by its founders and a German company. It has trebled in size in the past two to three years and this has put pressure on the culture resulting in significant staff turnover.

The CEO is fully supportive of rectifying the issues, and Frank is currently seeking a suitable coach/consultant/trainer to help identify the correct intervention in order to reduce staff turnover and put the business on a more solid footing regarding culture and people.

At the moment, there is no long-term written vision (ten-year vision) or clear purpose or values and associated behaviors.

Recommendation

My recommendation at this early stage is to meet James, the CEO, and find out what he wants and needs for the business. It's essential that James feels he can work with me and that his team would talk to me before I make any kind of recommendation regarding the proposed work.

Next Steps

Table 2.1 Next Steps

What	Who	By When
Write up an Update Note	RB	4 October
Set up a meeting with James	FJ	18 October

Follow Up

Your follow-up for Players on the Pitch is likely to come in the form of additional coaching and consulting particularly if there are changes to be made at the board or leadership level. This can be in the form of a group session to iron out differences or identify strengths.

It could also be in the form of additional training, such as 21st Century Leadership.

It might be that the business discovers a lack of talent in which case you might be helping them to recruit, first identifying the role clearly and next recruiting for values and not just skills.

Finally, you are more than likely going to help your client write clear job descriptions, with associated behaviors and support them to embed these into the business. Writing new types of job adverts may also be involved, as these will need to focus on values and behaviors as much as skills.

You are essentially helping the business bring their cultural and commercial side into balance one project at a time.

A Real-Life Example

A professional services firm is still using a form of Players on the Pitch four years after I introduced it. Every six months they update it to reflect their growing business.

Figure 2.2 Players on the Pitch QR Code.

Chapter 3

Economic Engine

Revenue Cycle

The Revenue category features other models such as:

- Business Development

    - Influence and Persuasion
    - Negotiation

Business development, influence and persuasion, and negotiation are not included in this book. My brother, Nick, and I are co-writing a book which specifically helps business coaches generate business. The subject was too large to include in this book.

Our course Thinking Big (really big) can also be included in the Revenue function of the business. It's ideally suited to developing the mindset of sales teams and business coaches! I have included it in this book because as a business coach and consultant, you're going to need it for your own development. It is yet another course that can be delivered over a series of months for your clients too.

Thinking Big (really big) has its own chapter. For now, here's the Economic Engine Model (Figure 3.1). Let's focus on this.

I've been in sales all my life and not once had I ever seen a complete revenue cycle that included the purpose, vision, and values of the business I was selling for. As my coaching and consulting work progressed, I heard many, many times from many different business owners and leaders that their sales teams 'just didn't get it.'

The sales teams would be battered, bullied, and blamed for the lack of sales coming into the business by the boss. I would go and speak to those sales people and ask them what was going on. Sure, there were some people who were a bit lazy and didn't put in the calls or meetings needed to make the sale. Most were really hard working and keen to make the sale but lacked clear direction and the words to use with their prospects to make it easy for them to buy.

Hence, the Economic Engine was born.

DOI: 10.4324/9781003540694-3

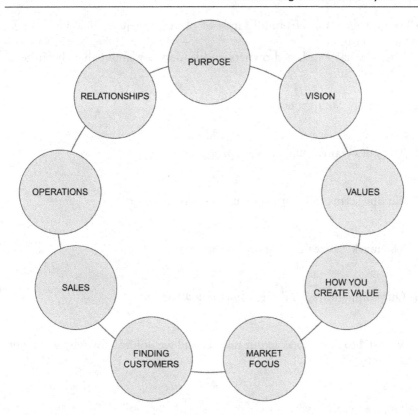

Figure 3.1 Economic Engine Model.

Once I've helped the business to establish it's Purpose, Vision, and Values, it becomes easy to use the words in the Values Grid (see Culture as a Foundation for Growth) to speak to prospects about the product or service.

It also becomes easier to use these words in bids, tenders, presentations, talks, and exhibitions. In fact, these words appear everywhere. Wherever there's a written document, speech, social media post, etc., these words are used to convey the message the business wants to send.

Let's crack on and show you how to use this nifty little model.

This is another model I use in ten-minute chats over coffee, free hour-long workshops, half-day and full-day workshops.

It's another one of those simple tools that wins you brownie points with your prospect or new client and gives them real value in real time, really quickly.

Let's start with the things I usually hear clients talking about when they tell me about their revenues. I'll use the word 'revenue' throughout the book as opposed to turnover or sales. This is because the revenues from a business can come from all kinds of places, not just sales. It's a more inclusive term.

This is what I've heard owners and leaders say about their businesses over the years:

1 We simply can't generate more sales

#

2 The sales team aren't working properly

#

3 No one seems to be buying our products or services

#

4 The market is really tough at the moment

#

5 Our competitors are doing something we're not

#

6 We used to be the best in our market and we don't know why we're not anymore

#

7 We need more revenue and fast

#

These are the questions I'll ask the client:

1 How would generating more sales enable you to grow the business or enable you to do what you can't do now?
2 What's changed in the marketplace in recent times?
3 How has the business adapted to those changes?
4 How are you looking after your existing clients, especially when they're not buying?
5 What levels of revenues would you like and by when?
6 I could do some sales training, but am I sure that this is the real problem?

Point six isn't a question. I'm sure you've spotted that. I've added it in because many clients come to you with a presenting problem. Let me reassure you, that the problem is never the problem. The problem they tell you about is the very end result of the major problem that is sitting somewhere up the chain of command in the business. It's your job as a business coach and consultant to find the 'big, ultimate' issue or issues.

Now you know what's bothering your client, you know it falls into the Revenue category and you can show them the Economic Engine Model.

The first three circles are taken care of in Culture as a Foundation for Growth, so I'm not going to go over those. Your client needs to have these pieces of the puzzle in place before you tackle any of the next circles in the model. If they tell you they have these in place, ask them where it's written, ask them if it's included in their ads, bids, tenders, content, marketing materials, induction process, and appraisal systems.

If it's not, they don't have them in place and you have another project on your hands!

Back to the rest of the nine circles.

Circle 4 – How You Create Value

It's astounding how many businesses haven't thought about whether they're a service- or product-driven business. It's even more astounding how many sales teams don't know this either.

During coffee with prospects, I ask them if they consider their business to be product or service driven. Most of them stop and look up to the ceiling for inspiration before answering ….

"Hmmm, great question. I think we're mainly service, but we do have some products."

I know at that point, I've got my work cut out.

You cannot hope to maximize revenues unless you know whether you're selling a service which usually takes time or a product which is usually quick. Don't make this complicated, simply ask your client if they know the names of their client's pets (if they're calling them clients, they're likely to be running a service-based business) or where they go on holiday.

If they know the answer to these questions, their business is highly likely to be service based. Even if they make a product, the level of service required to deliver that product leans toward a service-based way of selling. For example, Porsche turned their fortunes around when they realized people bought from them because of the service, they happen to make amazing cars too so the product has to back up the service.

On the other hand, I know law firms that have created products such as an HR package based on a monthly fee. Their clients get a fixed number of hours, with fixed products they can access at any time and the law firm can build volume. At this point, the lawyers don't know the names of all their client's pets and have no idea where they go on holiday. The process of onboarding is transactional. This makes it a product-based business and the selling must be done in a product-focused way.

At Tricres, we made the decision to move from service to product when we created the Kick A** Culture Coach and Consultant Program online. We offer a great service around that product, but we lead with the product and I don't know the names of your pets. This book is part of our product extension offering. I still coach and consult and my brother still trains lawyers in global law firms, but this is now how we're building the business. We're leading with the product and so the way we sell had to change.

We can no longer meet every single one of our online purchasers for a coffee, most are in the USA or other end of the UK from where we live. We had to find a way to sell our online product in high volumes and that's when I had to learn the dark arts of digital marketing. That subject is not included in this book as I'm an enthusiastic amateur!

Circle 5 – Market Focus

Your client can run around targeting every man and woman and his or her dog to make a sale. This is exhausting and pointless. Your job is to help them decide where to focus.

There is more content in the online Economic Engine ground-level course to help you nail this with your client. Again, it's simple. Do they sell in high volumes or low volumes? Are their products or services expensive or cheap? If your client is an SME, they need a niche. They need to focus on a particular demographic, geography, interest, or style to be successful.

Why? You might be asking.

Think Amazon. They sell everything to everyone everywhere because they have a massive scale. Your average SME business does not have this and cannot service it properly. That's the reason they need to niche and get good in that niche. Other work and opportunities will follow from that niche as they grow. I promise.

At Tricres, we only want business coaches and consultants. We don't want life coaches, nutritional coaches, etc. We also only want business coaches and consultants who are a bit different. They don't like the norm and they see themselves as individuals who can think for themselves and are perhaps slightly rebellious (maybe that's just me!)

Once your client has Circles 1–5 nailed, they're well on their way to creating a brilliant, sustainable revenue cycle.

Circle 6 – Finding Customers

Because your clients have circles 1–5 under control, where they find their customers becomes obvious. You need to work with your client to find out where the people who share their purpose, vision and values hang out. These are the people who want the product or service your client is offering.

I recently interviewed a guy for my Entrepreneurial Journey podcast, you can check it out here https://tricres.com/podcasts, who designs products for people, who love games like Doom and films like Lord of The Rings. He hangs out at Comicon Conventions because that's where his target audience likes to hang out.

It seems obvious, but believe me, I've come across some business coaches who are hanging out in the wrong places and expecting to find their ideal clients.

Remember, hanging out on the right social media platform is just as important as hanging out at networking events and conferences. You've got to pick the right channel to focus on for your client base. Ours is on LinkedIn, so we conquered that before even thinking about any other platform.

Circle 7 – Sales

I don't talk a lot about selling because my big brother Nick (and co-founder of Tricres) is an expert in this field. If you want to take a look at his work, you can find him on our website www.tricres.com or wait for the book we're writing specifically aimed at business coaches and consultants like you. It will come out straight after this one.

Your client should have a good sales process in place. They should have a good Customer Relationship Management (CRM) system such as HubSpot, Pipedrive, or SalesForce, etc. They should know how long it takes to make a sale, where most of their sales come from, and what kind of outreach, cold calling, email campaigns, etc. work and don't work.

If they don't know this stuff, then you can do one of two things:

1 If your background is in sales, you can help them implement all of the tools and processes they need to be successful.
2 Help them recruit someone who can do this either on a permanent or freelance basis.

It's a good idea to have a few freelance consultants and coaches in mind for specialist areas such as finance, IT, HR, and sales if you don't have these skills in your toolkit.

In my experience, most of the businesses I've worked with have a good sales team and they just need some clarity on the purpose, vision, and values piece to get their pitch right. I tend to work with the heads of sales and marketing on this or the most experienced salesperson in the business.

After that, I leave them to it or get my big brother to come in and do some training in business development.

Circle 8 – Operations

Some of you will have great expertise in operations. I don't. Luckily, all my clients have had people with this kind of expertise in-house so I haven't needed to get involved.

However, if your client doesn't have this expertise, there are a few options available to you. If the business is relatively simple and there are obvious gaps in the process of getting the product or service to the client after they've parted with their money, then as a business consultant and coach you're likely to have some good ideas to help them smooth out the bumps.

Things I have suggested in the past are:

1 Aligning the CRM, sales database with their product catalog for instant dispatch
2 Approaching a logistics tech company to help with any manufacturing to the fulfilment process
3 Finding a new Operations Manager if there is already one in place and things still aren't working
4 Appointing an Operations Manager if there isn't one – what it costs in salary will be made up for in the delivery of product or service
5 Finding an external consultant who can help
6 Finding someone in the business with a good logical brain who loves creating systems and processes and can share that expertise.

There are probably a million and one other ideas. The point is, your role as a coach and consultant is NOT to do the work. Your role is to ask the questions that help your clients to uncover their own answers. Your questions should point them in the right direction and you can offer solutions which they may or may not take up.

Circle 9 – Relationships

This last circle is more important than you think. I once won six months' worth of work based on the ninth circle!

I'd taken the client through the other eight circles and they'd been able to answer most of the questions. When we got to circle 9, the client told me they had over 30,000 names, addresses, and contact details of people who had previously been clients. When I asked how they were keeping in contact with those people even though they weren't buying anything at the moment, the answer I got astounded me.

Not a single one of those 30,000 previous clients had been contacted at all. Not one.

It was only when I asked about how they kept in touch with people who were no longer buying from them (this is the question I always ask in relation to the ninth circle) that the client realized they had an enormous amount of potential revenue sitting there waiting to be realized.

Sadly, the founder of the business wouldn't listen and kept focusing on getting new clients, which weren't very profitable due to their business model and did not consider investing heavily in the 30,000 existing clients to be a worthwhile exercise.

Needless to say, the business eventually folded and was bought out by a competitor who no doubt made great use of the additional potential clients on their database.

It might be lunches, offers, newsletters, mailing lists, invites to events, presents, service reviews, site visits, free audits, competitions, prizes, podcasts, etc. These are the things businesses can send to or invite the clients and customers who have bought from them in the past. None of them is particularly expensive to do – unless you're chartering yachts, but so many businesses forget this part of their Economic Engine and lose profitable revenues.

Even if your work with your client only gives them one idea to convert old customers and clients into returning customers and clients, then you're likely to have paid for yourself.

Follow Up

You can see how the Economic Engine could be months' worth of work or an hour's discussion. Much depends on what the client already has in place. The first three circles are two days' work alone. After that, it could well be one day each for the other elements or more.

Use your skill and judgment as professional coaches and consultants to decide whether your client has this covered or needs your support to get profitable revenues flowing.

NOTE: Make sure your client understands which revenues are profitable. If your client doesn't have clear, accurate, and timely financial information, particularly monthly or quarterly management accounts, you need to find someone internally or externally who can provide that. Without this key information, your client is running blind. So are you. If your background is finance and accounting, this person might be you (I wouldn't recommend it as you'll get stuck in the weeds), if not, find a good freelancer or internal hire to make sure this is done and done fast.

A Quick Example

I conducted a Purpose, Vision, and Values session with an £18m turnover business back in 2023. They're an extremely well-organized and successful business, so after this initial piece of work haven't needed much from me.

I have coached and consulted with their heads of marketing and HR to help those individuals embed the behaviors into the various people and revenue systems in the business. This has meant a visit every couple of months over the past twelve months. Not a huge money spinner, but a good piece of work where the client has been able to establish a new language and approach to sales and marketing that has accelerated their growth.

The consistent language and acceptance of using their values to make decisions and embed their culture has meant the acquisitions they've been making have been much easier to blend into the existing business.

In particular, their tender documents now speak about their values and behaviors which has meant they're much clearer on their proposition and are winning more bids.

Figure 3.2 Economic Engine QR Code.

Chapter 4

Habits and Housekeeping
The Suite of Strategies for the Business

The Strategy category features other models such as:

- The Horizon Model
  - Habits and Housekeeping
  - Strategic Thinking Made Easy
  - OKRs Made Easy
  - Growth Accelerator
  - Players on the Pitch

Each of these has its own chapter.

Running a sustainable, ambitious business needs planning. Yes, there are some businesses that end up being successful despite the fact they wing it. These are the rare exceptions and you don't hear about the millions of other businesses that fail due to lack of good planning and organization.

My first business was a recruitment business. It failed. I didn't have a vision, plan, strategies, or good financial information. I had tons of sales, in fact the sales came too easily which is probably why I didn't plan properly. I just assumed we'd always make more cash.

When we stopped making cash, that's when I realized we didn't have a plan.

Habits and Housekeeping is about exactly that. Getting into the habit of having a plan, following it, reviewing it, and changing it when necessary.

The model is used as a checklist to make sure the business has the relevant strategies in place and is using them to grow. The nuts and bolts of writing those strategies can be found in Strategic Thinking Made Easy and OKRs Made Easy. You can also find some high-level planning tools in The Horizon Model. All of that information is included in this book.

Like so many of our foundational models, Habits and Housekeeping can be used in a ten-minute chat over coffee all the way up to a five-year plan in a larger business.

DOI: 10.4324/9781003540694-4

HABIT	STAGE 1 Our business understands the idea	STAGE 2 Our business has a written plan for this	STAGE 3 Our business is actioning this strategy	STAGE 4 Our business has a feedback and review mechanism	STAGE 5 Our business knows and understands its secret sauce and is using it to grow
Project management					
Managing money					
Strategy					
Structure					
What we're worth					
Marketing					
Finding customers					
Sales					
Operations					
Relationships					
Culture					
Succession planning					
Future growth					
How we create value					
JV / Partnerships / Collaborations					
Scalability					
Brand development					

Figure 4.1 Habits and Housekeeping Matrix.

The way to discover whether your client needs to focus on the development of a suite of strategies is to listen to the kind of things they're telling you. You've guessed it, these clues are featured in the main PDF workbook that accompanies the online course.

• We're busy doing so much these days, I'm not sure what direction we're going in
• We've lost focus
• We're not sure what we stand for anymore
• The last strategy failed
• We've never had written strategies
• We want to sell in a few years and need to build maximum value in the business
• I want to step back and hand my knowledge over to the next leader or owner
• I can't find the right senior people to run my departments

It's important to note that when a business has clear, written strategies, it knows where it's going, how it's getting there, and what to do when it gets there. This model also helps the business uncover its secret sauce. We'll get to that in a minute.

Now you know what's bothering your client, you know it falls into the Strategy category, and you can show them the Habits and Housekeeping Model.

The following questions are the questions you can ask your client:

1 Would I like to have a clearer idea of the direction of the business?
2 How quickly would you like to be able to step back from the business?
3 What's your timescale for selling the business?
4 When you find senior people, are they clear on what their roles, responsibilities, and accountabilities are?
5 How do you create more value in your business?

Whether I do this exercise with an individual business owner, leader, or a board of directors depends on how much time I spend on it. You can imagine running through this exercise with a board of directors will take half a day to a full day and just going through it one-to-one would take about an hour.

Much depends on the scale of the business and the number of heads of functions you need to speak to.

Stage One – Our Business Understands This Idea

You need a simple tick or cross in each box in this column. For example, if the person you're asking says 'yes,' the business understands the idea of 'People Management,' then you put a tick in that section under column one.

Go down the list and ask the person or people you're speaking to whether the business deserves a tick or cross for each item.

You should have a complete list of ticks in column one. Understanding the idea is pretty straightforward. You'll find the definitions of each section at the end of this chapter.

Stage Two – Our Business Has a Written Plan for This

In my experience, your client will have some ticks for this column and quite a few crosses. It's absolutely essential the business has a Written Plan (or strategy – same thing). If the plan is stuck inside the owner's head, then it's worse than useless. If the owner disappears for any reason, no one has a clue what's happening. You can imagine how this reduces the efficiency of the business and its value.

If there is a cross in any section under column two, then that category gets a cross in every column. The plan has to be written to deserve a tick.

Stage Three – Our Business Is Actioning This Strategy

This is where the ticks get thinner on the ground!

Even if the strategy is written, I find quite a few businesses that stick it in a file and forget about it. They revisit it a year later on their next "away day" and discuss the same thing again, wondering why they didn't achieve it last year.

This is usually because no one 'owns the strategy and no one is reviewing the strategy or measuring its progress. I wrote the OKRs Made Easy course to stop this from happening. At this point, my clients use to freak out because no one knew how to write a strategy, and then I wrote Strategic Thinking Made Easy.

Stage Four – Our Business Has a Feedback and Review Mechanism

I've given you an example of a strategy at the end of this chapter. At the bottom is the person who 'owns' it and what date it needs to be reviewed.

I then give you an example of a reviewed or updated strategy because guess what? Strategies are not written in stone. They are live documents which need to be amended according to changes in the markets, profits, and the economic, political, legal, tech, and social landscape.

Strategies that worked pre-Covid are highly unlikely to work today.

Getting your client to have regular meetings with clear agendas, clear outputs, and clear Next Steps is one of the most important habits you can get them into. My clients have regular board meetings, regular senior management team meetings, and regular reviews of their overall vision and business plan.

A good pattern for a small- to medium-sized business looks like this:

1 Annual strategic review with annual OKRs set (Organizational Key Results)
2 Quarterly review of strategies and annual OKRs (in OCRs Made Easy, you'll see the big annual OKRs are broken down into smaller quarterly ones, one quarter at a time)
3 Two weekly update on OKRs' progress of quarterly OKRs
4 Monthly board meeting with key financial information, management accounts, and key operational, people, revenue matters.

If your client has this in place already, that's fantastic. If not, you might want to get involved in the annual and monthly sessions to make sure they stay on track. I do this with some clients and charge them for it. I also send them the relevant Update Note after each session and refer back to the Next Steps they said they were going take.

It's business coaching and it works.

Stage Five – Our Business Knows and Understands It's Secret Sauce and Is Using It to Grow

If you have a client who has ticks across all columns for a particular section, then it's highly likely you've hit on their secret sauce.

What do I mean by 'secret sauce'?

It's the thing a business does in a particular way that other businesses in that sector aren't necessarily doing in the way they're doing it.

For example, I had a cracking construction company client. The way they trained apprentices was exceptional. They had ticks across all the columns for Succession Planning because they took apprentices from school and trained them in their way of working. One such apprentice had recently taken over as MD of the business after twenty years.

Other companies have done the same. One is a cleaning contractor and the current CEO started in payroll. The company's strategy around succession was so good, it meant she could work her way up to the top. She's now a shining example of what's possible in the business.

These organizations could well share this expertise with the world and create separate profit centers. They could create a training academy or offer their training to other organizations.

Tricres did this. We worked out a way to download the contents of an owner's brain and create a set of courses for a learning platform. We did it ourselves first, got a system, and then charged a client to do it for them. We're not taking this any further, but it just goes to show what secret sauces sit inside businesses ready to be used to create more profitable revenues.

When I've worked with clients on this, there's a great 'ah ha' moment in the room when they realize they've got stuff they take for granted every day that could be used to expand their business.

Follow Up

The key to following up on Habits and Housekeeping is keeping in touch. If you're working with the client on other projects or have been invited to attend their monthly or quarterly meetings, this becomes easy.

If you haven't, then a 'hands-off' approach is needed. I do this by checking in with the owner or leader of the business on the other projects they're working on. My contract cleaning client is very well organized and doesn't need me much. However, we are working together to embed the behaviors across the business and roll out their purpose, vision, and values. To date, I've seen the head of HR and marketing together to roll out the plan and more recently had an update with the CEO.

I'm keeping them on track and offering support where needed. Our next meeting isn't for another few months, but I'll charge them for that and make sure they deliver.

With other clients, I'm there every month, sometimes twice a month to do this. Much depends on the capacity and capabilities of your clients. Be of value. Don't be there for the sake of it. You'll win more clients by being honest and saying 'You don't need me right now' than trying to muscle in on things where you're just not needed.

Business coaching and consulting isn't about you. It's about your client.

Definitions of Each Section

Table 4.1 Definition of Terms in Habits and Housekeeping Matrix Competency

People Management	**How you manage people in your business, e.g., this might include an organizational chart as well as managerial and leadership style**
Managing Money	How the business manages its finances
Strategy	**How the business designs and implements strategies and what the overall strategy is for the business, e.g., the Purpose, Vision and Mission**
Structure	Is it a limited company, LLP, LLC, Corp, or partnership, does it have a board and senior team?
What are we worth?	**How do we formally place a value on our business? Is it fee income, income per head, assets, IP, etc.**
Marketing	What is our marketing strategy and how does it support our Purpose, Vision, Values and Mission?
Finding Customers	**What are our channels to market? Do we sell directly or through distributors?**
Sales	What are our sales objectives? How do we sell as a business? Online, face-to-face, or both?
Operations	**What are our operational plans? How do we deliver on our confirmed sales?**

(*Continued*)

Table 4.1 (Continued)

Relationships	What kind of relationships do we want with our clients and our suppliers? What are our promises to our employees?
Culture	**How do we do things? What underpins us? What behaviors do we expect?**
Succession Planning	How do we bring new people in and up through the business? How do we make sure we have good people who can eventually run the business?
Future Growth	**What plans do we have for growth in two and three years? How will we achieve our ultimate Vision?**
How we create value?	Are we a product- or service-led business? What do we have in our business that's magic?
JV/Partnerships/ Collaborations	**Are we a business happy to collaborate? Will we grow through JVs or partnerships or will we be doing this on our own?**
Scalability	How do we scale this business? Do we want to?
Brand development	**How does our brand promise compare to our vision, values, etc. How do we consistently deliver on that promise to our external and internal customers? How will our brand grow as we grow?**

Example Strategy

An Example of a Strategy

Here's an example of a succession planning strategy for a family-run business turning over around £4m to £8m.

The revenue of the business is not important. It's the way the business will be run when the current CEO, owner, or MD steps down or steps back that's important.

If you're just starting your business, you will need to understand how it will operate without you at some point, so it's still worth to have a succession strategy. It's just one you'll probably leave until you're better established.

Purpose: To transform the way legal firms communicate
Vision: To work with a passion for tech and people
Mission: To be the best in the UK at what we do
Values: Clear, concise, advanced

Strategy for a Succession Plan

Objective

Our founder, Gary will be ready to retire in ten years and we want to make sure the business has a strong senior management team (SMT) from which we can choose his successor. We'd like to be able to be spoilt for choice among the SMT.

Process

All our people processes are designed to develop the full potential of each person in the business, and we already have the following in place:

- A clear induction program
- Regular performance reviews and personal and professional development training
- Internal recruitment processes to encourage promotion from within the business
- A career plan for everyone in the business
- Stretch targets for those who want to progress rapidly

We now want to introduce a Leaders of the Future development program to ensure we have a number of leaders from different areas of the business, who can potentially develop into the role of CEO and continue to grow with the business.

Leaders of the Future Program

This will be developed with the Board of Directors and HR. Competencies, behaviors, and attitudes will be identified that are desirable in the CEO of the future.

People interested in this program will be encouraged to apply by completing an application form and attending an interview and conducting a presentation around their ideas for growing the business.

A coaching and training program will be offered to those people who are identified as Leaders of the Future, using external consultants and coaches when needed and setting up a mentoring program within the business.

Outcomes

It is envisaged that up to five people will be on the Leaders of the Future program which will run every two years, giving people the opportunity to apply even if they're new to the business and allowing for those who may decide to move on from the business.

We anticipate this building a strong core of highly competent individuals who are aligned to the culture of the business and who will be suitable candidates for progression to either the senior management team or the board.

Budget

A further £10,000 will be allocated per year to the learning and development budget to facilitate this process.

Review and Ownership

This will be reviewed every six months to ensure it's working well and achieving the objectives.

Margaret, our current head of HR, is fully responsible and accountable for the leadership and delivery of this program.

Example of an Updated Strategy

An Example of a Strategy
  Amended (bold)
  Here's an example of a succession planning strategy for a family-run business turning over around £12m.

The revenue of the business is not important. It's the way the business will be run when the current CEO, owner, or MD steps down or steps back that's important.

If you're just starting your business, you will need to understand how it will operate without you at some point, so it's still worth having a succession strategy. It's just one you'll probably leave until you're better established.

Purpose: To transform the way legal firms communicate
Vision: To work with a passion for tech and people
Mission: To be the best in the UK at what we do
Values: Clear, concise, advanced

Strategy for a Succession Plan

Objective

Our founder, Gary, will be ready to retire in four years and we want to make sure the business has a strong SMT from which we can choose his successor. **We have a very strong SMT and we want to select the best person to succeed Gary from this team if possible.**

Process

All our people processes are designed to develop the full potential of each person in the business, and we already have the following in place:

- A clear induction program
- Regular performance reviews and personal and professional development training
- Internal recruitment processes to encourage promotion from within the business
- A career plan for everyone in the business
- Stretch targets for those who want to progress rapidly
- Our Leaders of the Future program has been a big success and we now have a very strong talent pipeline in the business

We now want to create a good Executive Development program and select the best candidate for the CEO's role, whilst keeping the candidates who are unsuccessful motivated and within the business if possible.

Executive Development Program

This will be developed with the Board of Directors and HR. Competencies, behaviors, and attitudes will be identified that are desirable in the CEO of the future and will be fit for a business that moves into revenues of £25m – plus with acquisitions likely.

People interested in this program will be encouraged to apply by completing an application form and attending an interview, and conducting a presentation around their ideas for growing the business.

We anticipate applicants will pursue further personal development as well as professional development opportunities, including external courses and, qualifications, and engaging with an executive coach.

Outcomes

It is envisaged that up to three people will be on the Executive Development program which will run every two years, giving people the opportunity to apply even if they're new to the business and allowing for those who decide to move on from the business.

We anticipate this building a strong core of highly competent individuals who are aligned to the culture of the business and who may be suitable candidates for progression to CEO.

Budget

A further £30,000 will be allocated per year to the learning and development budget to facilitate this process.

Review and Ownership

This will be reviewed every six months to ensure its working well and achieving the objectives.

Lynda, our HR Director, is fully responsible and accountable for the leadership and delivery of this program.

Figure 4.2 Habits and Housekeeping QR Code.

Chapter 5

Growth Accelerator
Measuring the Stages of Growth

The Strategy category features other models such as:

– The Horizon Model

  – Habits and Housekeeping
  – Strategic Thinking Made Easy
  – OKRs Made Easy
  – Growth Accelerator
  – Players on the Pitch

Each of these has its own chapter.

The Growth Accelerator is based on the formula used to value businesses, namely, value equals profit times multiple

$$V = P \times M$$

If profit is the part of the business accountants are interested in and manage, then the multiple is the part of the business we, as business consultants and coaches, are interested in enhancing.

Imagine a business that has an average value. At Tricres, we refer to this as 'the pink line' because our model has a pink line in the middle of it.

Everything below the pink line (or the average value of that business in that particular sector) is related to the finance and accounting function.

These elements are:

• Cost management
• Revenue control (we call it Economic Engine control)
• Asset management
• Management of liabilities
• Economic and political landscape

DOI: 10.4324/9781003540694-5

The last element cannot be controlled by finance, but a business can make financial provision for uncertain times.

Sitting above the pink line are the elements that add to the multiple of the business. The multiple is the number by which someone valuing the business will calculate the value by multiplying the profit and the multiple.

The following elements are included in the multiple:

1 Talent pipeline, quality senior management team, culture, and strategies (at Tricres we call this Habits and Housekeeping)
2 Innovation
3 Product and service extensions
4 New channels to market/partnerships/joint ventures
5 Brand architecture
6 Scalability

As business coaches and consultants, it is important to remember you are adding value by strengthening the elements above the pink line. I've specifically numbered these elements because you must tackle them in the correct order. It's impossible to build scale if you haven't got the other elements in place first. This is exactly why we call our culture piece Culture as a Foundation for Growth. It is very hard to achieve sustainable growth without a clear, positive, well-defined culture.

This is the knowledge I wish I'd had the first time I set up and ran a business.

If I'd known that the secret to building the value of a business was to focus on developing a senior team, building a powerful culture, and developing a suite of strategies that were being implemented, I would have been a lot more successful sooner.

I'd also love to have known that you need to build these things before you start messing about with innovation, product and service extension, joint ventures, and brand architecture. I tried to scale before I had any of this in place and it failed.

The second time around, I got all the foundational pieces in place, then innovated until I got a great product market fit, then started adding on product extensions and a joint venture, and now we're into building the brand architecture. This guide is part of that brand architecture!

I've repeated the information here because it's so important. Many business owners are skeptical about engaging with business consultants and coaches, particularly ones that talk about culture. They think it's woo woo. When I tell business leaders their businesses could be worth up to seven times the average value for their sector, they tend to sit up and listen. Even if they don't achieve that kind of increased level of value, they will build stronger, more sustainable businesses by having these elements in place.

The pink line on the diagram (shown as a grey brushstroke here) is the baseline value of the business. It represents what the market will generally pay for a business in that sector. The market works out the value using the following equation:

THESE ARE THE THINGS THAT CREATE UP TO 7 TIMES THE AVERAGE

VALUE OF YOUR BUSINESS:

- Scalability

- Brand Architecture

- New Channels to Market/Partnerships/Joint Ventures (JV's)

- Product and Service Extension

- Innovation

- Talent Pipeline, Quality SMT, Culture and Habits and

  Housekeeping

Figure Ten

Figure 5.1 Things That Create Value.

$$V = P \times M$$

At Tricres, we're in the business of building the multiple. The accountants take care of the profit and we build the value of the business, which is everything above the pink line. Accountants deal with everything below the pink line.

Make sure your client gets a decent bookkeeper and accountant on board. Please make sure all your clients have such people in place, even part time. There are so many outsourcing organizations now that even the tiniest business can afford this service.

Now your client has their numbers sorted … and by sorted, I mean: invoicing, receiving payments regularly, paying taxes, etc. your clients now need to be building their businesses from the inside out.

If they're already established, you can use the Growth Accelerator as a quick and dirty measure of how well placed they are to succeed.

Do they have a clear, identifiable culture? If yes, then you need to find where they have that embedded and how it's reinforced, delivered, etc. in practice. If not, go back to Culture as a Foundation for Growth and deliver the one-day Purpose, Vision and Values workshop. Then follow the process to roll out and embed.

Does the business have a strong senior management team (SMT)? If yes, then that's fantastic, you just need to find out who they are and what they're accountable and responsible for using Players on The Pitch.

If they don't have a strong SMT, then you need to propose putting their senior leaders (often including the board) through 21st Century Leadership. See the end of this book for the agendas or sign up for the Kick A** Culture Coach and Consultant Program if you haven't done so already.

Finally, do they have a good, solid set of strategies that are being implemented? If yes, then great, get copies and find out whether they're on track or if these documents are just collecting dust. You also need to find out who is responsible and accountable for delivering on them and how often they're reviewed. This is all in Habits and Housekeeping, which we've just covered.

If the answer is 'no,' nothing is being planned, nothing is written down, and no one really knows what they're doing; then you need to support the business by helping them write such documents.

This could be a-day workshop, using Habits and Housekeeping and OKRs Made Easy. It could be done one-on-one or could be delivered as part of the 21st Century Leadership Program.

Either way, you need to get the business to the point where it has a clear annual strategy, clear strategies for each area of the business, and someone needs to be responsible and accountable for writing and delivering on those strategies.

It might look something like this:

The Board – CEO owns the overall business strategy

Finance Director owns the money management and how the business is valued strategy
Sales and Marketing Director owns the sales and marketing strategy
HR Director owns the people, succession planning, and talent strategies, and possibly culture too

As you go down the organization you may have heads of functions or senior managers who are accountable and responsible for a section of the strategy, for example
Sales & Marketing Manager – owns the online sales & marketing strategy

Financial Controller – owns the credit control, debt management, and professional qualifications strategy

HR Manager – owns the policy and procedure strategy

I wouldn't go any further down the hierarchy than senior managers unless it's a huge organization and needs additional layers of leadership.

Keep strategies simple. They are just a plan.

Make sure you only have three key objectives for the year and these feed into your objective for each quarter – see OKRs Made Easy.

Keep on top of it.

I've seen businesses wander off in all kinds of directions because they didn't keep tight control of this stuff.

Use the Growth Accelerator as a conversation piece to highlight which area of the business needs attention first. I use it if the owner doesn't want to do a full Fact Find. I use it to shape a conversation with the board or leader about what's in place and what isn't.

You can also use the grid in a free talk or free seminar for your audience to complete and give themselves a score (as I write this, I'm about to deliver a keynote talk to fifty construction business owners on this very topic and hand out a copy of the Growth Accelerator PDF!)

Here are some of the things you might hear when your client needs the Growth Accelerator:

1 What could my business be doing that it isn't?
2 Are we fit for the next three years or do we need to make changes in structure, people, skills or even products and services?
3 Do we have a succession plan or talent pipeline?
4 How are we managing our sales cycle?
5 We seem to be going around in circles and I'm not sure why
6 We feel stuck
7 I am exhausted, and my heart isn't in it anymore
8 We've got incredible plans for growth and aren't achieving our potential.

Here are some questions you can ask your clients:

1 Do you want to do things differently to achieve growth?
2 Are you prepared to invest time, money, and resources into growing?
3 Do you view this as an investment or as an expense?
4 How much time are you prepared to dedicate to this?

Finally, the score card.

THE GROWTH ACCELERATOR AUDIT

BUSINESS ELEMENT	SCORE /10	WHAT	DETAILS DISCOVERED DURING AUDIT	RECOMMENDATIONS	PROGRAMME TO USE
CULTURE					
1. Purpose		What is the reason for the business' existence?			Culture As A Foundation For Growth
2. Mission and Vision		What change are you trying to bring about with your business and what is the nearest horizon line you're currently working towards?			Culture As A Foundation For Growth
3. Values		What are the stated values and how are they used to make decisions in the business?			Culture As A Foundation For Growth

BUSINESS ELEMENT	SCORE /10	WHAT	DETAILS DISCOVERED DURING AUDIT	RECOMMENDATIONS	PROGRAMME TO USE
TALENT					
1. Talent Attraction		How are you attracting the best talent into your business?			Talent Attraction And Succession Culture As A Foundation For Growth
2. Talent Retention		What are you actively doing to retain that talent?			Talent Attraction And Succession Employee Engagement Performance Management 21st Century Leadership
3. Talent Development		How are you actively developing the talent you already have within your business?			Talent Attraction And Succession Great Team Development
4. The Right People In the Right Roles		Are there decisions to make about moving people on, up or out?			Players On The Pitch

BUSINESS ELEMENT	SCORE /10	WHAT	DETAILS DISCOVERED DURING AUDIT	RECOMMENDATIONS	PROGRAMME TO USE
BRAND					
1. Internal view		How do your people perceive your brand?			Developing a Brilliant Brand
2. External view		How is your brand perceived by your customers?			Developing a Brilliant Brand
3. Positioning		How are you positioned in the market place you currently operate in?			Developing a Brilliant Brand

BUSINESS ELEMENT	SCORE /10	WHAT	DETAILS DISCOVERED DURING AUDIT	RECOMMENDATIONS	PROGRAMME TO USE
INNOVATION					
1. Product or Service Extension		What do you currently have that you can create differently?			Our Economic Engine and Building a Brilliant Brand will help you with this
2. R&D		Is there someone focussing on research and development in your market?			Our Economic Engine and Building a Brilliant Brand will help you with this
3. Leveraging our Secret Sauce		This is about HOW you deliver your product or service. In what way do you do it differently in your market place and how do you promote that? If you were to know what to do differently, what would this be?			We find that our Tricres Coaches can spot your secret sauce more easily than you can, just because we see so many businesses and know how things are done elsewhere. Contact us to find out about engaging with one of our highly experienced coaches hello@tricress.com

Figure 5.2 Growth Accelerator Scorecard.

BUSINESS ELEMENT	SCORE /10	WHAT	DETAILS DISCOVERED DURING AUDIT	RECOMMENDATIONS	PROGRAMME TO USE
CHANNELS TO MARKET					
1. Collaboration and community		Who are you working with? How is that working out?			Our Economic Engine will help with this
2. Partnerships and JV's		What formal partnerships and or JV's are there now or in the pipeline?			Our Economic Engine will help with this

BUSINESS ELEMENT	SCORE /10	WHAT	DETAILS DISCOVERED DURING AUDIT	RECOMMENDATIONS	PROGRAMME TO USE
SALES					
1. Revenue Generation		Do you understand the need you're meeting in the market? Are there any blockages to growth?			Our Economic Engine will help with this
2. Tools to sell more		How are you selling? What CRM are you using?			Our Economic Engine will help with this
3. Marketing campaigns		Are you selling to the right audience in the right way?			Our Economic Engine will help with this

Figure 5.2 (Continued)

Use this to sit down with your clients or ask them to complete them on their own or as a board. This will give a quick and dirty version of the Fact Find and is useful when clients want to work faster or don't have the cash to pay for a full Fact Find.

I don't use it that often, because most of my clients opt for the Fact Find. It's a handy tool though. You can also use it when you've been working with a client for a while to monitor progress.

You might consider using it as a FREE health check or Growth Audit for your clients as a way to demonstrate value. It's a nice piece of kit that could well help you get your foot in the door.

Figure 5.3 Growth Accelerator QR Code.

Chapter 6

The Horizon Model

Business Planning

The Strategy category features other models such as:

- The Horizon Model
  - Habits and Housekeeping
  - Strategic Thinking Made Easy
  - OKRs Made Easy
  - Growth Accelerator
  - Players on the Pitch

Each of these has its own chapter.

The Horizon Model is another simple model with a powerful impact.

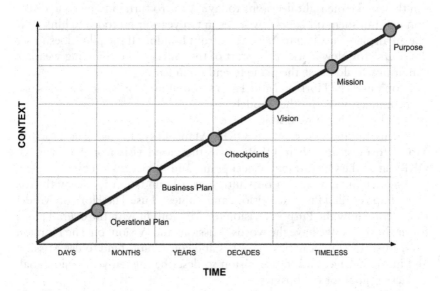

Figure 6.1 The Horizon Model.

DOI: 10.4324/9781003540694-6

It is best used as a high-level conversation tool or a quick planning tool in conjunction with Strategic Thinking Made Easy and OKRs Made Easy.

We all know that in order to plan a project you need to start with the end in mind.

Exactly the same principle applies to a business. Most businesses are started because the founder is frustrated with something and wants to create something better. At this point in time, very few people are thinking about their exit.

This is understandable when there are no customers, there isn't a bank account or even a domain registered.

However, sitting down with a coach or consultant (like you) to really think about where the business wants to go and what the business is going to do for you is probably the best investment any business owner will make in the early days.

There are many well-established businesses that have never thought of this. I've worked with businesses that have been established for fifteen years and the owner is reaching sixty years old and they still haven't thought about an exit.

As a coach and consultant your role is to ask your clients about the decisions they're making today and how those will impact them and their businesses in three, five, ten, and even twenty years from now.

The Horizon Model is the tool that helps you get that conversation going.

If your client doesn't know where their business is going, how the heck can they make the right decisions today? A micro turn in the wrong direction will put them off course by miles in ten years from today. Think of it like an airplane heading to New York from London. If the pilot doesn't set the course for New York at the start of the journey, the changing weather conditions could cause the plane to end up in Rio!

I don't use The Horizon Model as a stand-alone workshop. I always use it in conjunction with other models.

Let's break that down, so it's clear.

When running a session on OKRs Made Easy, I'll use The Horizon Model to illustrate where OKRs sit in the grand vision of the business. OKRs sit at the Operational, Checkpoint, and Business Plan bit.

When running a session on Culture as a Foundation for Growth (the workshop is called Purpose, Vision, and Values), I use The Horizon Model to illustrate how the Purpose, Vision (or Mission) fit with the overall plans for the business. We have the words 'Mission' and 'Vision' on The Horizon Model because our American coaches and consultants tend to use Mission and in the UK we tend to use Vision to describe the ten-year vision/goal/ audacious goal for the business.

The Purpose is eternal and shouldn't change for the business. It might be modified over time, for example, Tricres began life as a traditional coaching and consulting business so our purpose was to make it happen for every business on the planet.

That remains our purpose and we're now delivering that by training business consultants and coaches like you to deliver our methodology to your clients. Plus, we're also making it happen for your business too!

As we discussed in Culture as a Foundation for Growth, Purpose has to be timeless. It's also vague and has a huge amount of emotion attached to it.

These are the things your clients might be saying which would indicate that The Horizon Model is worth talking about:

- We seem to be doing ok but have no idea how we got here
- I'm not sure what the future holds for our business
- I have no idea why this vision and purpose nonsense is worth doing
- If we just focus on the here and now, everything will be ok (except it isn't ok really)
- People are telling me they don't know what the business is about or where it's heading
- One of my best senior managers has just resigned because she/he doesn't know where the business is going
- We take one step forward and two back
- There's no excitement around here anymore
- All we seem to do is bang on about KPI and I've no idea why

When talking to your clients about The Horizon Model, you can introduce some of the tools in this book. Hopefully, this will lead to more work for you and better outcomes for your clients.

If your client has no purpose, mission, or vision, you can suggest a Purpose, Vision, and Values workshop. This is found in Culture as a Foundation for Growth.

If your client lacks checkpoints, a business plan, or operational plans, then suggest Strategic Thinking Made Easy and OKRs Made Easy. I would also add that if all these things are missing, you'll need to take the board and leaders through 21st Century Leadership to understand leading themselves, leading people, and leading the business thoroughly. There's more of that at the end of this book.

Figure 6.2 The Horizon Model QR Code.

Chapter 7

OKRs Made Easy

Organizational Key Results

The Strategy category features other models such as:

- The Horizon Model
  - Habits and Housekeeping
  - Strategic Thinking Made Easy
  - OKRs Made Easy
  - Growth Accelerator
  - Players on the Pitch

Each of these has its own chapter.

Of all the systems for keeping track of objectives, goals, and plans, Organizational Key Results is the one I've found the easiest to understand, use, and implement with clients.

This is a simplified version of the spreadsheet you can use to measure OKRs. I give my clients a copy of a spreadsheet with two sheets. One is for the Company's OKR and the other is for the individuals in the team.

I first learned about OKRs from a client. I think we learn the most useful things from our clients. When you hear something good from your clients, go and check it out. That's what I did for OKRs.

Company OKRs	Individual OKRs	How is it calculated?	How often do we measure it?	Comments	Base Value	Target Value	Current Date and Current Value	Progress	1 Sept	1 Oct
Objective 1	Objective 1									

Figure 7.1 OKR Grid (Simplified).

DOI: 10.4324/9781003540694-7

I discovered that OKRs were born in Silicon Valley among the tech giants. Most of my clients are tiny compared to such huge organizations, but the principles of OKRs work well with individuals and multinationals.

As with almost all of our content, we've tested them for ourselves here at Tricres. We run our business using OKRs and it means we get a lot of stuff done for such a small team. I firmly believe this is due to two things:

1 We've got a brilliant culture which is truly embedded
2 We use OKRs religiously!

If you're with us as a coach and consultant, you'll know we get you to set your OKRs and we hold you accountable.

I turned it into a workshop and added it to the 21st Century Leadership training when a client was struggling to get their senior managers to write strategies and implement them. One cohort on 21st Century Leadership commented that the OKRs Made Easy session combined with Strategic Thinking Made Easy was the best session of 21st Century Leadership.

OKRs Made Easy can be used as a stand-alone half-day workshop or as part of 21st Century Leadership in Modules 5 or 6.

If your client is struggling to meet its targets or hasn't got clarity on direction or objectives, this is a great workshop to use with them.

We provide you with editable OKR spreadsheets that your clients can use in their businesses in the online course, but can't do that in a book! We advise you, as coaches and consultants to use these for your own business too. If you're signed up for our Kick A** Culture Coach and Consultant Program, we ask you to set three big goals for the year (moonshots) and then three for the first quarter.

OKRs encourage people to aim high, so when you're working with your clients, please encourage them to pick objectives they're going to find difficult to reach. These must be aspirational. Some of you may say goals have to be realistic. At Tricres, we politely agree to differ on this matter. We set aspirational objectives, targets, etc. because that's where the learning can be found. The juice is always in the journey.

There's no learning happening when you happily plod along to reach a perfectly realistic goal. It becomes boring and too easy to achieve. At Tricres, we aim high and if we reach a high result, we're pleased and then wonder whether it was too easy. If we don't reach a high result, we know we've got more work to do and there's a better way of doing things.

The same goes for your clients. Their learning, growth, and innovation will stem from aiming high.

I've implemented this in a couple of businesses and watched a business implement this system for themselves. The warning I have for you all is your clients will try and overcomplicate it. It's a very simple system that works. Sometimes your clients won't quite believe that such a simple system actually works. It does and they need to keep it simple.

Here's how it goes:

1 Set three key objectives for the business to reach at the end of twelve months, make them measurable and have a starting point you can measure against. Record this in an editable OKR spreadsheet
2 Set three key objectives for the first quarter of the business. Put that in the spreadsheet too with the original figure or starting point.
3 Each person in your team will set their own three objectives for twelve months and record it on the spreadsheet. They own these and decide what they are for themselves. This is the whole point of OKRs, people own their objectives and take full responsibility for them.
4 Every two weeks get together for thirty to forty-five minutes and discuss where you're up to with your results.
5 At the end of the quarter, review where everyone is at and compare to their twelve-month objectives. Also, look at the whole business' objectives and see whether you're on track
6 Set new objectives for the next quarter
7 Repeat the process
8 At the end of the year, review all objectives and give a final measurement for the business and each person. Set the new objectives for the next twelve months and repeat the process.

Moonshots and roof shots. Moon shots are your big, audacious objectives and roof shots are the ones you're likely to get. Be happy with one or two moonshot achievements and the rest are likely to be roof shots.

Be aware that the modern business landscape changes all the time, so you'll need to tweak some of your objectives as you go. Not all can be measured with numbers, so get creative.

Nothing is cast in stone. Your clients need to understand things change and so their OKRs will change over time.

The bi-weekly meetings should be short and to the point. It's about supporting each other to succeed and offering encouragement or empathizing when things don't go according to plan. There should be no blame or telling off during these meetings. The OKR process is a positive one which helps the business to remain on track, keep going when the going gets tough and remember what it's supposed to be doing even when the world around it may seem chaotic.

We've designed questions to ask about OKRs Made Easy, even though your clients are unlikely to specifically use the term OKR. Your conversation is likely to be around goal setting or strategy. Here are some things to think about when you're listening to clients:

Do they set goals each year and never achieve them?
Do they have problems getting their senior team to deliver on objectives?
Does the business have objectives or milestones to achieve?
How does the business measure those milestones?
When was the last time the business reviewed its goals and objectives?
Does the business overcomplicate its objectives?

There are many more questions you can ask about goals, objectives, and reaching milestones. These are the ones to get you started.

Example of OKRs Working in the Real World

I'm going to use the example of the client who originally introduced me to the concept of OKRs. They ran with it for a while, then dropped it. About two years later, they picked it up again and are still running with it today because it means they get a lot of things done with a relatively small team.

They dropped the system because they overcomplicated it. Another client of mine has done something similar. I attempted to embed it too early and they were confused. Once they realized that setting a strategy and keeping on track with executing that strategy was difficult, they then combined a form of the business model canvas (Google it) and OKRs to come up with their version of a business planning tool.

This often happens. Clients will take something and 'make it their own.' This is to be encouraged. It's a great sign that your clients have taken your support on board and are using it to great effect.

Figure 7.2 OKRs Made Easy.

Chapter 8

Strategic Thinking Made Easy

The Strategy category features other models such as:

- The Horizon Model
    - Habits and Housekeeping
    - Strategic Thinking Made Easy
    - OKR's Made Easy
    - Growth Accelerator
    - Players on the Pitch

Each of these has its own chapter.

This course does what it says on the tin. For some reason people find it hard to think strategically, so I've made it easy to learn.

Once upon a time, I did not think I was very good at strategic thinking.

Then, in a blinding flash of inspiration, I realized a strategy was simply a plan that you then delivered on. At the same time I realized this, I looked back over my life and noticed that I'd been planning things and then delivering on them since I was fourteen.

This revelation came when I was about forty-five, so I'd been a great strategic thinker for most of my life.

Essentially, if you can make a plan about what you'd like to happen in the future, write it down so someone else can read it and understand it and then do the things you've said you're going to do, you're a great strategic thinker.

Strategy is another thing that people in businesses like to over-complicate, so when the head of learning and development for a huge multinational asked me to design a workshop for twenty-four of their high-performing leaders, I jumped at the chance.

For those of you studying our Kick A** Culture Coach and Consultant Program, you'll notice I combine Thinking Creatively On Purpose with mind maps and the PATH diagram. This is to help your audience get

DOI: 10.4324/9781003540694-8

creative. Don't worry if you're not studying our Kick A** Culture Coach and Consultant Program because we'll get to PATH and Thinking Creatively On Purpose later in this book.

I think this is where most issues lie with strategy. People attempt to design a strategy from a cold, standing start. You need a bit of a warm-up to get your brain cells working in the right way before you jump in.

Anyway, the workshop went down a treat and I then used it in 21st Century Leadership for Module 6 when we got to leading the business. The head of learning and development said she'd never found anyone who could teach strategic thinking well until she met me! Now you have the very same tools in your toolbox to impress your clients with.

She's asked me back this year, so she wasn't just being polite.

I managed to squeeze this into a 2.5 hour session, but I'd prefer a half day so people can relax into things.

I always start with the explanation of a strategy simply being a plan.
I've given you the agenda I used, go ahead and use it if you wish.

09:30   Introductions, temperature check, and what you want to get from the session

I use the Helter Skelter as a temperature check (see Helter Skelter Model on the next page). Find out from everyone in the room how they're feeling. Make sure you give them the "I'm about to talk about feelings" before you do.

09:45   Where are you now?

Unpacking how you currently think strategically. I ask the room what they currently use to think strategically and give the following choices:

- Mind maps
- SWOT
- PESTEL
- Daydream/go for a walk
- Don't think I think strategically

I find out what is currently working for them and not working. I also want to find out what they think strategic thinking is or isn't.

These are the very simple model I'll share with them to allow them to practice moving their thinking from strategic, to operational and back again. This is detailed in the Constructive Conversations Chapter. It's incredibly useful to use when people are stuck. Bear in mind you may need to play around with different models with people in the room as some will find ones easier to use than others. TOP TIP: have plenty of colored pens available!

Performance and Emotion

How might these emotions be observed in the workplace?

1 Euphoria Elation Joy
2 Expectant Peaceful Inspired
3 Passionate Excited Anticipating
4 Focused Clear Purposeful
5 Believing Confident Knowing
6 Hope Optimism Faith
7 Content Happy Calm

8 Bored Complacent Indifferent
9 Frustrated Irritated Impatient
10 Pessimistic Disappointed Sceptical
11 Discourage Disengaged Disheartened

12 Worried Doubt Unsure
13 Overwhelmed Confused Stressed
14 Blaming Detached Dismissive
15 Judgemental Elitist Egotistical
16 Defensive Justifying Threatened
17 Resentful Bitter Aggrieved
18 Anger Jealousy Spite
19 Hateful Rage Revenge
20 Guilt Insecurity Regret
21 Fear Helplessness Anxiety
22 Depression Despair Shame

Figure 8.1 Helter Skelter.

Figure 8.2 SWOT Analysis.

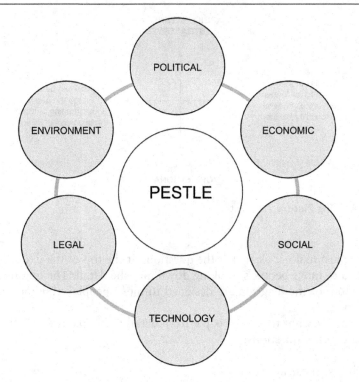

Figure 8.3 PESTLE Analysis.

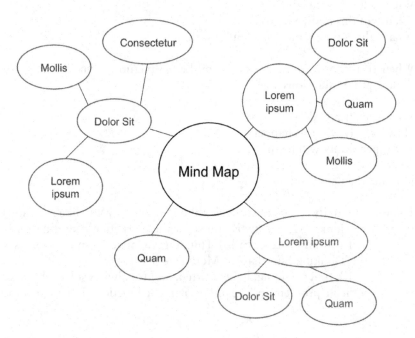

Figure 8.4 Mind Map.

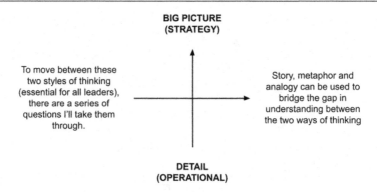

Figure 8.5 Big Picture and Detail.

You must make it clear that the questions at the top of the diagram are designed to move people's thinking down into the detail. The questions at the bottom of the diagram are designed to move people's thinking to the big picture.

When you want to move people from detail to big picture, ask the following types of questions:

For what purpose are you…?
For what purpose does this…?
What will this give you?
What will this allow you to do?
What's the ultimate outcome you're seeking?

When you want to move people from the big picture down to detail, ask these types of questions:

What specifically do you mean?
How exactly will this happen?
Who specifically will be there?

Give me the details on ….

10:00   Creativity is part of strategic thinking (whether you like it or not!)
Thinking creatively isn't just for the marketing department.
I run an exercise called Thinking Creatively On Purpose (see the Thinking Big Chapter, Module 4)
It's fun, engaging, light-hearted, and yet always solves the most difficult problem in a team/department function. It also gets the

group thinking with the less linear, logical, and rational side of their brains and into the imaginative, creative, and innovative side.

This works on the principle that no problem is ever solved in the same state of thought it was created in. Shift your state: solve the problem.

10:45   Coffee break
11:00   Use a real-life business example (or one from home if this isn't appropriate) to bring this thinking and the tools to life
        Present the scenario

- Ask the group to visualize where they want to finish up (know your outcome).
  If people get stuck on this (there are usually a few people who do get stuck), I have various techniques which help loosen their thinking and get them moving.
- Find out where they are now. They can use SWOT & PESTEL for this.
- Get them to work backward from where they want to be in twelve months – you can use PATH for this if you have time (see the Thinking Big Chapter, Module 4)
- Pop this information into a dashboard they can view at a glance

The full, editable dashboard is available in our Kick A** Culture Coach and Consulting Program.

Use this dashboard (see example dashboard on the next page) for review and monitoring of strategy

12:00   Review of outputs
12:20   Review of key learnings compared with objectives
        Questions
12:30   Close

That's how you use this workshop in the real world.

The questions you ask your clients to find out whether they need support with strategic thinking are at the end of the OKRs Made Easy chapter, here they are again to save you from looking them up.

Do they set goals each year and never achieve them?
Do they have problems getting their senior team to deliver on objectives?
Does the business have objectives or milestones to achieve?

Business Dashboard

Sector	
Month	
Date	
Version	

Target	
Billed	
% Billed to Target	

Key Actions	Key Activities	Value Proposition	Client Relationships	Our Client
Quarter 1 1. 2. 3. Quarter 2 1. 2. 3. Quarter 3 1. 2. 3. Quarter 4 1. 2.	What are our key activities?	What value do we deliver to our clients?	What type of relationship do our clients expect us to establish? What do we need to do to maintain relationship?	From whom are we creating value? What are our most important customers/potential customers?
3.				
Key Partners Who are the key partners we need to work with?	**Key Resources** What key resources do we need to deliver our value proposition?		**Channels** How do we reach our clients and help them evaluate our value proposition?	
Cost Structure Key costs in our business model			**Revenue Streams** How do we create revenue and maximum revenue?	

Figure 8.6 Business Dashboard.

How does the business measure those milestones?
When was the last time the business reviewed its goals and objectives?
Does the business overcomplicate its objectives?
I love this workshop, when everyone gets it, the scales fall away from their
    eyes!

Figure 8.7 Strategic Thinking Made Easy QR Code.

Chapter 9

Constructive Conversations
How to Communicate Effectively

The People category features other models such as:

- Employee Engagement
    - Talent Acquisition and Retention, Succession Planning
    - Performance Management
    - Constructive Conversations
    - Great Team Development
    - Culture as a Foundation for Growth

Each of these has its own chapter.

This was the first model I created.

At the heart of every culture in business sits communication. At the very core of great communication are conversations that happen between people. This model was born from my desire to understand my coaching approach. Someone asked me what my approach to coaching conversations was and this is what I came up with.

The background to this approach stems from my Neuro-linguistic Programming (NLP) training. It starts with 'earning the right' to have the conversation, that is, building rapport and ends with real, tangible outcomes. I'll explain the rest in the next section.

I use Constructive Conversations in 21st Century Leadership, Modules 2 or 3. I also use it in Great Team Development and in any communication workshop I might be delivering.

Figure 9.1 Constructive Conversations Model.

DOI: 10.4324/9781003540694-9

It's at the foundation of our Kick A** Culture Coaching and Consulting methodology and it's a model I encourage all leaders, salespeople, and anyone who needs to communicate anything to another human to employ. It's a simple model and it goes like this...

1 Get rapport with the people or person you're speaking to. This is simple, all you need to do is listen to them and then ask them questions about themselves. Use this tip in networking situations too.

   Because you're listening, you'll hear certain words or phrases they like using. Build rapport by repeating one or two of these back to them. DO NOT mimic them or repeat everything word for word because you'll sound like an idiot. This is about sprinkling your communication with one or two words or phrases they've said.

2 State the purpose of your meeting, session, workshop, conversation, etc. Simply state why you're there, and how much time you've both got and be honest about what kind of outcomes you're hoping for, this might go something like this...

   'Hi, thanks for taking the time to meet me today, I've got our meeting in the diary for an hour, is that still ok with you?'

   Pause and check it's ok.

   'Great, I'm hoping by the end of this I'll have a clearer idea of what you and your business need right now.'

   It's as simple as that.

3 Intake. Ask a question – one at a time please and then shut up and listen. This is where listening like a rock with ears comes in and where you might want to check out our learning platform to hear me talk you through Otto Sharmer's four levels of listening.

   If you're not signed up yet, here's the model Otto uses for listening.

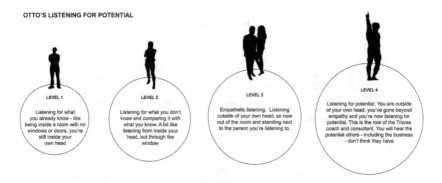

OTTO'S LISTENING FOR POTENTIAL

LEVEL 1
Listening for what you already know - like being inside a room with no windows or doors, you're still inside your own head

LEVEL 2
Listening for what you don't know and comparing it with what you know. A bit like listening from inside your head, but through the window

LEVEL 3
Empathetic listening. Listening outside of your own head, so now out of the room and standing next to the person you're listening to.

LEVEL 4
Listening for potential. You are outside of your own head, you've gone beyond empathy and you're now listening for potential. This is the role of the Tricres coach and consultant. You will hear the potential others - including the business - don't think they have

Figure 9.2 Otto Sharmer's Four Levels of Listening.

If you only practice one thing as a business coach and consultant, it's this!

I've also added some more questions here, so you can practice the Intake stage.

Tell more more about....

I'm curious to know how you want to....

For what purpose did you choose to...?

What will this give you or allow you to do...?

Who else?

What else?

Where else?

When do you want to...?

When did this occur...?

If you were to know, how would you...? (use this when you hear "I don't know")

What would happen if...? (use this when people say they can't)

How about...?

Describe to me....

When was the last time you felt good, confident, in control, etc.?

Have you done this before?

What do you need?

4   Clarify and understand. This bit of the model is about you asking a few more questions to get a bit more detail.

When you use this with clients, be sure to include the big picture and detailed questioning techniques. We saw some in Strategic Thinking as a way to move people from the big picture to detail and from detail to the big picture.

The same principles apply in everyday conversations. It's the best way to get absolute clarity of what people are saying.

Here's the big picture/detail model again.

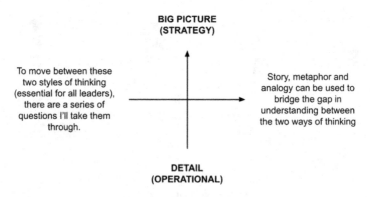

Figure 9.3 Big Picture and Detail.

Use some of these questions which are also statements of a kind to make sure you've grasped exactly what has been said in the conversation you're having. It's important to get this stage right as you can't possibly agree on Next Steps until everyone knows where they're up to.

These are more specific questions, which may lead you into some greater detail.

So, if I understand it correctly......

Am I right in thinking that...?

When you say "X" what do you mean exactly...?

Can you help me understand "X" in more detail, please...? Can I just check that...?

What would happen if...?

Is it a bit like...? – using metaphors, stories, and analogies to gain understanding is a very useful thing to do as everyone can grasp a metaphor, story, and/or analogy. If they don't understand or relate to your metaphor or analogy, people will translate it into one of their own. Here's an example:

I was working with a technical IT person and a designer, attempting to understand what they were both saying to me. It helped me to clarify by suggesting that the IT person was like the electrician or plumber in a house-building project and the designer was like the project manager and interior designer.

This helped me enormously and everyone else understood immediately what their roles were in the project.

Here's a great question bonus question to finish this section on.

Is there anything you think I should have asked and haven't?

5 Suggestions and solutions. Depending on the context, you might want to offer some suggestions or solutions to your audience or you might want to wait for them to come up with some. In a coaching scenario, I want my clients to come up with solutions. In a group/business coaching scenario, they might not have the answers because you might be with people who don't know what they don't know. This is where you have to offer suggestions or solutions.

Never 'tell' always 'offer.' I like to remind myself of my yoga teacher in this situation. She always 'invites' us to take up a pose, she never ever 'tells' us.

There is a subtle, yet important difference. Your options might be, 'You could' or 'Why don't you have a go' or 'You're very welcome to...,' etc.

Somehow, 'you must' or 'you have to' don't land well with clients!

6 Next Steps. This vital last step is often missed in conversations, meetings, etc. It's where people in the room commit to doing something by a certain time. I live, breathe, and die by this. I absolutely insist all my clients have this as part of their update notes after each session. Most of the time I have some Next Steps to carry out and they almost always have some too.

Take the Next Steps to the next session and do a recap – this helps keep everyone on track.

Next Steps look like this as in Figure 9.4.

What	Who	By When

Figure 9.4 The Next Steps.

This is what your clients might be saying if their business cannot have great conversations.

No one listens to a word I say
I just can't get through to people
The appraisals are a waste of time
I hate having performance conversations with people
Giving feedback is difficult, especially when it's not very positive
We're always at cross purposes
Our clients aren't happy because they say we're not listening to them
We need to increase sales
We need better meetings that produce real results
If you're encountering conversations that aren't working either in your clients' businesses or your own, learn our Constructive Conversations model.
Use this model often! Practice it in your own business.

Figure 9.5 Constructions Conversations QR Code.

Chapter 10

Great Team Development

The People category features other models such as:

- Employee Engagement
  - Talent Acquisition and Retention, Succession Planning
  - Performance Management
  - Constructive Conversations
  - Great Team Development
  - Culture as a Foundation for Growth

Each of these has its own chapter.

No one can build a business without having a great team with them.

At the heart of every clearly, identifiable, positive culture is a great team.

Building a great team is an art and a science. You need to keep an eye on the individuals in the team and the whole group of people who make up the team. It's not an easy thing to get right, but when you do, magic happens. When people come together in a team, they can move mountains, build business empires, and create massive change.

The contrary is also true. When a team disintegrates, it can be devastating for the individuals within the team and those around it.

Some of the best teams inspired me to write this course. Those include the teams who come together at short notice as a crew to fly and ensure our safety on planes as we travel around the world. The pilots and crew more often than not have never met each other before getting on the plane. They must work quickly and efficiently together to make sure the flight is both safe and comfortable for the passengers on board.

The other great teams I've read about and learnt from are those surgical teams who carry out life-saving operations, often under the most intense pressure. They come together quickly, efficiently, and calmly, each knowing exactly what their role is and who is in charge of bringing about life-saving surgery for the patient.

DOI: 10.4324/9781003540694-10

Finally, I've seen military teams working together. One of my earliest experiences in the workplace was visiting an army barracks in York. I was putting an assessment program together for railway signal design engineers and wanted to use the barracks for our team development element of the assessment.

I arrived, rather nervously as a twenty-three year old and was met in a very polite, efficient way by the Duty Sergeant on site. He took me to the Major's office, where I was immediately put at ease, made to feel comfortable and was given a tour of the facilities. Every single person in the barracks knew exactly what their roles and responsibilities were. They had respect for the Major and they had respect for themselves and their environment. It left a lasting impression on me.

Building a great team, and investing time, energy, and money into doing that is a really smart investment for any business.

Your role as a coach and consultant is to support them to do that as a part of embedding their cultural values and behaviors.

I draw from Patrick Lencioni's great work, "The Five Dysfunctions of a Team" If you haven't read it, please do.

I built on what he did and created my model, taken from a positive viewpoint. I look at what works to make a great team. My whole coaching approach is about what people 'can' do rather than can't do. I combined Maslow's Hierarchy of needs with this approach and this is what I came up with.

Great Team Development is a workshop. I usually deliver it over a full or half day, depending on the number of people in the session.

I use it as part of the 21st Century Leadership Program in Modules 3, 4, or 5 depending on where everyone's up to. In particular, I usually follow this pattern of delivery.

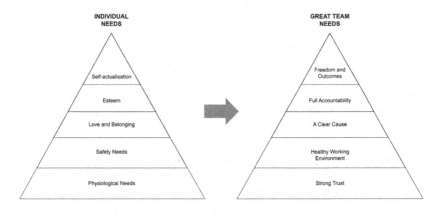

Figure 10.1 Great Team and Individual Needs.

Module 3 of 21st Century Leadership or a Stand-Alone Team Day

The first part of team development is about noticing where the team is at right now.

If I'm running Great Team Development as a stand-alone workshop or as Module 3 in 21st Century Leadership, I'll start with these concepts.

Let's find out where the team is up to on its development. I use Truckman's classic model, you're probably familiar with it.

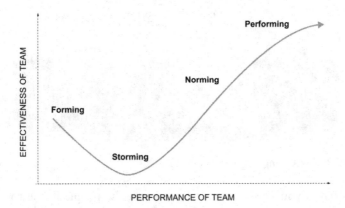

Figure 10.2 Tuckman's Model.

When delivering 21st Century Leadership, I ask the group to look at the phases on the curve and mark where they think their team sits and I ask them to think about the leadership team and mark where that sits on the curve. It's at this stage the people in the room make comments about having never thought of themselves as in a leadership team.

There's a great downloadable PDF in the Kick A** Culture Coach and Consultant Program that gives you more detail on this model, in particular how leaders should be conducting themselves at each stage of the team's growth.

The next part of the team diagnostic is the change house. I introduce the Change House in the team development part because it's often changes in the team that people notice first. If Truckman is an insight into the individual team, the Change House is an insight into the business as a whole. The business is still a team.

Again, there's a fully downloadable PDF available on the Kick A** Culture Coach and Consultant Program to describe this in detail.

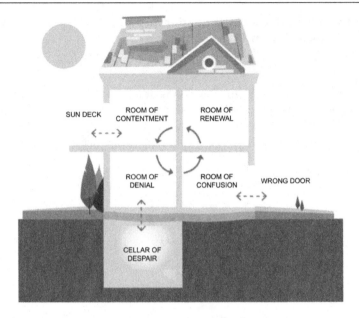

Figure 10.3 The Change House.

Essentially, you need to understand where the people in the room see the business in relation to the Change House. Are they in the room of denial for example? I often give examples of the old-fashioned, corporate record labels which were thrown off guard by freely available download-able music. Or the example of Blockbuster Video which ignored streaming services. Both types of business models were so big and comfortable, they got wiped out by the upstarts with new technology.

This is usually the point at which I say that the most dangerous phrase in business is, 'We're ok, it's worked well for us in the past, why should we change now?'

The room of despair is often when a business realizes it needs to change or die. This is when the leaders need to step up, take control, and make some clear decisions based on a clear vision for the future. It's often a time when the word 'pivot' comes into play. I don't like that word, but it's commonly used so everyone understands it.

Then there's the room of confusion. This is my favorite room. It's the room people often dread the most. I reassure everyone I'm working with that this is a great room because after confusion comes clarity. Or, in the case of the Change House Model, Renewal.

Whenever I'm working with clients and they feel confused, I ask them to embrace it and welcome it because they'll experience clarity very soon.

By this time, there's usually a great deal of discussion around change, teams and how people react to change, etc. As a facilitator of this session, it is up to you to notice the themes that pop up and observe how people are talking about their team, the leadership team, and change in general.

Remember, if you've already done the purpose, vision, and values work with the business, you've got their values grid, behaviors, and supporting systems grid to refer to during this session. This helps your groups shape their thinking around the kind of behaviors they want in the teams they're developing.

Modules 3 or 4 or 21st Century Leadership and the Next Part of a Stand-Alone Great Team Development Workshop

I use the model of the tree to make sure everyone is clear on what the differences between behaviors, beliefs, attitudes, and values are.

The Tree Diagram

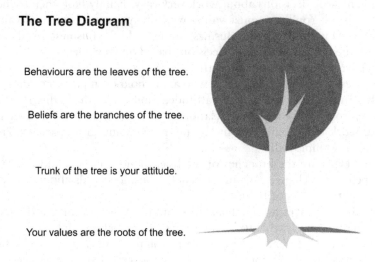

Behaviours are the leaves of the tree.

Beliefs are the branches of the tree.

Trunk of the tree is your attitude.

Your values are the roots of the tree.

Figure 10.4 The Tree Diagram.

When I introduce the idea of giving and receiving feedback. Most people are terrified of giving and receiving feedback. I've lost count of the number of times I've run this exercise and seen huge shifts in relationships between people within teams.

The first shift I usually observe is when they finally see themselves as a team. Often, boards and senior management teams don't view themselves as a team. It's only when they realize they have to run the business together and work together to do that they suddenly consider themselves to be a team.

Here's a quick guide to The Tree Diagram.

Explaining this helps people understand they're only giving feedback on behaviors and not the person's core personality.

Essentially, the roots are considered to be the values of the human being. Those values have been built since birth through the parenting, environment, upbringing, teaching, religion, community, and friendships the young person has experienced.

The values are fairly fixed, they may wobble during adolescence, but the young person usually comes back to the foundations built during their upbringing.

Values can change suddenly due to illness, a near-death experience, trauma, divorce, or the death of a loved one. An example of this might be someone having a core value of work. The death of a loved one or near-death experience may well make them change that value to family.

Mine are family, social life, and business. As soon as I decided on these, it made making decisions about work very easy. Family first, then friends, then business. You'll recognize values with the purpose, vision, and values work we do with businesses. Business values hold the business steady and secure. The business can make decisions based on its values.

At Tricres ours are: bold, impactful, and direct. We live and breathe those values, never working with people who aren't bold or impactful or direct.

The trunk of the tree is your attitude, similar to values, this is about your approach to work, love, relationships, money, health, etc. I have a strong work ethic, built into me by my parents and grandparents. They were all self-employed!

The beliefs are the branches of the tree, these can come and go. Even large beliefs can change. Again, the beliefs a business holds about itself can be crucial to success or failure.

Finally, the leaves are the behaviors and when we're running the feedback exercise, this is what we're focusing on. This helps people understand they're not doing a character assassination on their colleagues, they're simply talking about behaviors. Because behaviors can change, while keeping values in tact, this is what we use to give and receive feedback.

You must set the context for your clients when you run the feedback exercise and use the information I've just given you. Running the feedback exercise 'cold' may result in some upset!

The feedback exercise is this.

Ask everyone what the single most important behavior they display that adds to the success of the team.

Then ask, what the single most important behavior they display that detracts to the success of the team.

Again, there's more detail on our learning platform. Everyone has a turn in answering those questions about their colleagues and writes the answers down. You do this one at a time and you start with the most senior person in the team. Everyone listens to the answers and the person who is receiving the feedback may write things down, but not comment until the end.

Run properly and in a good-humored way, this exercise can be a game changer.

This exercise can take up to two to three hours depending on the number of people in the team. Take breaks if you have a large group. I have run it on Zoom and it worked well. It is better in person though.

Module 4 of 21st Century Leadership or Part of a Stand-Alone Great Team Development Workshop

If you've got a whole day with a team, this next part can form part of that agenda for a stand-alone workshop. If you're delivering the team development part of 21st Century Leadership I'd use the next bits for Module 4.

This is a team diagnostic. Again, there's much more detail on our Kick A** Culture Coach and Consultant Program, but here are the key principles.

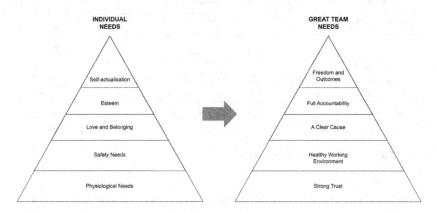

Figure 10.5 Individual and Great Team Needs.

A great team needs to be built on strong trust, then a healthy working environment needs to be in place, the team need a clear cause to follow, full accountability, and finally, freedom and clear outcomes so there's a sense of ownership and achievement.

The following questions are designed to help your participants measure these things, I ask participants to allocate scores to these questions on the following scale:

1 = Rarely
2 = Sometimes
3 = Usually

SECTION A	1. If a team member does make a mistake or say something that causes conflict, then they're happy to apologize and the team is able to move on		
	2. Team members are open and honest about the irmistakes or weaknesses		
	3. There are friendships amongst team members and people take a genuine interest in each other's lives outside of work		
	5. Team meetings are held in engaging, purposeful way and result in action	TOTAL A	
SECTION B	4. Members of the team can talk freely about what really matters		
	6. In team meetings, difficult issues are laid out on the table and dealt with effectively and with the right kind of health debate		
		TOTAL B	
SECTION C	7. Everyone in the team knows what everyone else is working on and where they're all heading		
	8. When team members leave a meeting, they are sure that everyone is committed to the agreed course of action, even if there were heated discussions in the meeting		
	9. Discussions amongst the team end with clear, decisive actions that are carried out		
		TOTAL C	
SECTION D	10. Members of the team can spot underperformance or unacceptable behaviour and speak to each other in constructive way about it to correct it		
	11. Members of the team do not want to let their team members down		
	12. Members of the team are happy to challenge each other on assumptions, decisions and outcomes in a healthy, constructive way		
		TOTAL D	
SECTION E	13. Sacrifices are made by team members such as giving up time, reallocating resources or compromising for the good of the team		
	14. When the team doesn't meet their objective or goal, morale tends to suffer		
	15. Members of the team enjoy giving other team members credit for success and don't try to take all the glory		
		TOTAL E	

Figure 10.6 Great Team Diagnostics.

There are the instructions on the online program in the downloadable PDF. I usually print out the whole Great Team Development document professionally and hand it out to everyone in the room. Printable copies of all Tricres courses are available here: https://fuelmybusiness.mykajabi.com/offers/6LuVq5vj

The scores slot nicely into this model.

A score of 8 or 9 is a probable indication that your team is getting everything it needs to thrive.

A score of 6 or 7 indicates that the needs of the team are being partially met.

A score of 3–5 is probably an indication that the needs of the team are not being met and there could be issues that need resolving.

Depending on the results in the room will depend on what you do next in the workshop.

If you've already carried out the feedback exercise, then I suggest you move on to developing the communication part of team development. That comes in the form of building strong communication skills and at this point, I'd return to Constructive Communications for a refresher. Or,

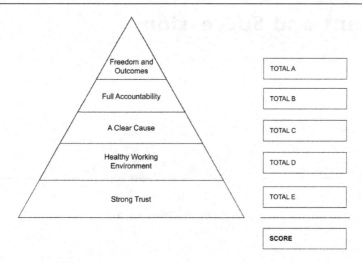

Figure 10.7 Triangle Scoring Model.

if you feel you've covered that in enough detail, I'd use the free diagnostic tool we call How Do You View the World?

This is a simple and very unscientific tool we use to help people understand their communication styles. I often use it in Team Development days and in 21st Century Leadership, usually in around Modules 4 or 5.

It's in our Kick A** Culture Coach and Consultant Program for this as it's far too detailed to explain in a book! The link to The Great Team Development online course, including our How Do You View the World Questionnaire, is at the end of this chapter.

Extras

If I'm delivering Great Team Development as part of 21st Century Leadership, this is where I'll finish. If I'm delivering Great Team Development as a stand-alone team workshop, I'll add in the Thinking Creatively on Purpose Exercise and PATH diagram in the afternoon session at the end of the day. Both of those are in Thinking Big which has a whole chapter dedicated to it.

Figure 10.8 Great Team Development QR Code.

Chapter 11

Talent and Succession

The People category features other models such as:

- Employee Engagement

  - Talent Acquisition and Retention, Succession Planning
  - Performance Management
  - Constructive Conversations
  - Great Team Development
  - Culture as a Foundation for Growth

Each of these has its own chapter.

When working with leaders and boards of directors, it became apparent to me quite quickly that not everyone had thought about who was going to take over the running of the business when the current owners/leaders had retired or left the business.

People seemed to be so busy running the business, they'd forgotten to nurture and develop the people coming up the ranks. This issue comes into stark reality when you run the Players on the Pitch model at the start of your working relationship with your client.

Running that model enables the owners to see that most of the accountability and responsibility lies with them. The question of 'what happens if you're run over by a bus tomorrow' always comes up. There are usually some blank looks, followed by 'erm, I'm not sure.'

This is when you know the business you're working with needs to start building the capabilities of its people working their way up the business.

Even if the owner claims to never want to leave the business, you still have the issue that one day they will die. This is when the question of legacy crops up. If the owner you're working with insists they'll be working in the business until the day they die, then you need to find out what kind of legacy they want to leave.

DOI: 10.4324/9781003540694-11

Most business owners will acknowledge that they do need to prepare the next generation of leaders to run the business when they're gone. In all the years I've done this, there has been only one leader who would not face up to the fact that he would not be running the business from his grave. Sadly, that business went bust and the owner is still at a loss as to what to do with his time. This is one example of why having work as your first core value is not a good idea.

Most business leaders see the need to develop the people coming up behind them, if only so they can start delegating some of their massive workload and focus on building the business!

Here's our simple model for tracking talent.

NURTURING TALENT AND SUCCESSION PLANNING MODEL

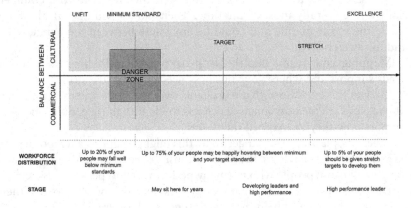

Figure 11.1 Talent and Succession Tracking Model.

Talent attraction is about getting your culture right. If your client is asking about attracting talent to their business, your first step is to ask about their culture. Very few people move simply for a higher salary. Once a person has earned enough for their desired lifestyle, more money isn't usually the main attraction to a business.

The main attraction is culture.

Once a business has got its culture sorted out (hopefully, thanks to working with you), it needs to set about keeping and nurturing that talent.

This course can be used as a stand-alone session. It is also used in 21st Century Leadership, Modules 4 or 5.

Everything you do with your client or a business does on its own, should be aimed at making sure the organization has a good balance of cultural and commercial skills, behaviors, systems, and strategies. When a business has leaned too much into the culture, not much work gets done. Read the story of Zappos written by its founder (now sadly deceased) Tony Hshieh.

If you're going to get a balance across a business, your people need to have that balance too.

The chart is simple. Take each member of your team and place their name on the scale. For some people, their names will need to appear twice. For example, Doris might be brilliantly culturally, so she'll sit at the top block of the chart toward excellence. However, commercially (skills, technical ability, selling, etc.), she sits in the danger zone in the lower block of the Model.

Bobby might be well balanced both commercially and culturally, in which case his name sits along the black line balancing nicely between commercial and cultural attributes and more than likely in the target-to-stretch zone.

The same goes for Puneet, Zoe, and Stef, they're great both commercially and culturally most of the time. Their names will appear along the black line in the middle and could be anywhere between the danger zone and the stretch area.

Mapping your teams like this helps to understand where each person needs support and where your business needs to add strength.

I've run this exercise with a few clients over the years and each time they sit back and tell me how much easier it is to identify those people who need support now they've mapped them out.

When people are in the danger zone, this might be due to a temporary setback in their personal lives, health, relationships, etc. Death, divorce, illness, etc. can all cause people who normally perform well to perform less well.

Each business will know their people best and will be able to give them the time, support, and help they need to get back on track.

Sometimes though, you just get people who are never going to work out. That's ok. Not everyone you hire will fit in or meet your standards. It doesn't make them bad people, it just makes them not right for your business. Please have sensible conversations with such people and make sure your client has given these individuals every opportunity, the right training and support they need to make improvements.

If, over time, those improvements aren't made, then I'm afraid it's a case of letting that person go. As a coach and consultant, you may need to support your clients to make this decision. Always, always, always get professional HR/legal advice for your clients. Unless you are an HR professional yourself and your qualifications are up to date with the latest employment laws, never give your clients advice on how to hire or fire people.

Even if you hold a professional HR qualification, I would advise you as an external coach and consultant that getting involved in this kind of process is getting too close to your client.

Having identified your client's talented individuals, it's then up to you to help your client nurture and map that talent to create a succession plan.

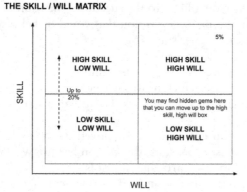

THE SKILL / WILL MATRIX

Figure 11.2 The Skill Will Matrix.

Just before you do that though, here's the second part of the people puzzle.

When you're thinking about the talent in your client's business, you also need to help them think about the skills and the will of the people in their business. If you think about it, most people come to work wanting to do a good job and will need a bit of training and support to work at their best. There are a few, highly talented people who will excel with little support or training.

There are those people, as we saw earlier, who might fall into the danger zone from time to time. These people may lose the will to work at their best for a whole variety of reasons. Hopefully, they can be nurtured to come back to high-skill and high-will performers.

There are those people who have 'checked out.' They can do the job well, but they're only really doing half-heartedly. In a big corporation, they can hide for quite a long time. In a small to medium-sized business, there are fewer places to hide and the business can't usually afford to carry these people.

That's when the HR conversations have to kick in and performance has to be managed.

When you're delivering this as a stand-alone workshop (half a day is likely to be sufficient), there will be lots of discussions, questions, and chats about what to do with people who aren't performing. My answers are usually non-directive enough to get the message home....

I ask my clients the following questions:

1 How much time and energy is being taken up with this individual's performance?
2 Have any of your interventions, support, training, etc. led to a sustained improvement?

3 What is this person adding to the success of the team/business?
4 Is this person taking up a position that could be held by someone who can perform to a higher standard?

The client will answer these questions and decide for themselves. In my experience, clients are reluctant to sack people (it's not easy to do in the UK and much easier to do in the USA) because they partly see it as a failure on their part.

This is true to an extent. They employed the individual in good faith and for a whole host of reasons, this person has not worked out. It might not be anyone's fault, in particular, it just is.

One thing is for sure though, if your client doesn't do something about underperforming staff, their business is going to struggle to succeed because the high performers will leave in light of inaction around underperformance.

Mapping the Behaviors through Your Client's Business....

Do you remember way back in Chapter 1, Culture as a Foundation for Growth, we added a list of behaviors that were aligned with the values?

Here's a quick recap.

The next part of talent and succession is where you support your client to build out the behaviors so they're embedded across their People Systems.

In true Tricres style, we use a cake as our model!

Values Grid

VALUE	MEANING	BEHAVIOUR	SUPPORTING SYSTEM
Bold	• Brave • Fearless • Challenging	• We stand by what we say • We say it as it is • We are leaders	• Our branding and marketing • Our growth plans • International expansion
Impactful	• Disruptive • Inspiring • Empowering	• We challenge the status quo • We instill belief • We make it happen, quicker	• Our learning platform • Our coaching, consulting and training methodology • Our lack of bureaucracy
Direct	• Agile • Creative • Game-changing	• We are flexible • We think outside the box • We deliver WOW results	• Each partner learns a new skill every year • We welcome feedback in all of its forms • We are avid readers, consumers of relevant expertise in all its formats

Figure 11.3 Values Grid, Complete.

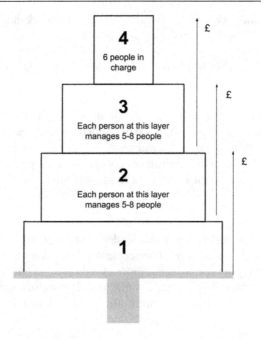

Figure 11.4 Cake Model for Behaviors.

At layer one, your client will list all the behaviors that are expected in their business as a minimum. Layer 1 is an entry-level job in their business.

Layer 2 is the next level up and will include all the baseline behaviors AND new ones to reflect the additional responsibilities at the next level in the business.

Layer 3 repeats layers 1 and 2 and adds further enhanced behaviors again representing the additional responsibilities and accountabilities at that level.

Layer 4 is the final level (although, I have had clients who have got six layers in their business) and will include the board of directors.

Here's an example taken from our downloadable PDF in the Kick A** Culture Coach and Consultant Program.

Layer 1

Entry level into the business
Standard Behaviors (this is a minimum for your business)

- Open to learning
- Enthusiastic
- Positive attitude
- Open to feedback and learning from it

- Easy to get along with and adds value to the office/workshop environment
- Happy to take on basic tasks

Stretch Behaviors (this is when you start identifying the person for your talent pipeline

- Goes out of their way to learn something new in their own time
- Offers to support other people's work when under pressure
- Remains cheerful during stressful times
- Displays resilience when customers complain or they receive feedback
- Comes up with new ideas or ways to improve the business

Layer 2

The first level up: supervisor, team leader, shift supervisor, workshop, or shop supervisor, also first level management roles. Likely to have responsibility for direct reports or working more closely with clients/customers and likely to be empowered some make some everyday decisions in the business.

Standard Behaviors (this is a minimum for your business)

- Open to learning
- Enthusiastic.
- Positive attitude
- Open to feedback and learning from it
- Easy to get along with and adds value to the office/workshop environment
- Good with customers/clients and flexible in their approach to problems
- Offers support and gives feedback and praise when needed

Stretch Behaviors (this is when you start identifying the person for your talent pipeline

- Goes out of their way to learn something new in their own time
- Offers to support with other people's work when under pressure
- Remains cheerful during stressful times
- Displays resilience when customers complain or they receive feedback
- Comes up with new ideas or ways to improve the business
- Actively encourages others to learn and develop
- Goes the extra mile for customers and clients

Layer 3

This layer consists of experienced managers and senior managers as well as deputy directors or heads of functions that report to a board.

Standard Behaviors (this is a minimum for your business)

- Open to learning
- Enthusiastic
- Positive attitude
- Open to feedback and learning from it
- Easy to get along with and adds value to the office/workshop environment
- Good with customers/clients and flexible in their approach to problems
- Offers support and gives feedback and praise when needed
- Is able to identify and nurture talent in their team
- Creates a great team working environment
- Is a strong communicator both internally and externally
- Good problem solver

Stretch Behaviors (this is when you start identifying the person for your talent pipeline

- Goes out of their way to learn something new in their own time
- Offers to support with other people's work when under pressure
- Remains cheerful during stressful times
- Displays resilience when customers complain or they receive feedback
- Comes up with new ideas or ways to improve the business
- Actively encourages others to learn and develop
- Goes the extra mile for customers and clients
- Is innovative in their thinking and can generate new revenue-generating ideas for the business
- Has a good grasp of the strategic direction and vision of the business and can communicate this to their team effectively
- Also able to contribute to the strategic direction of the business

  1 If you're running this as a workshop session, encourage your attendees to work on the first two
  2 layers of behaviors and then take the rest back to the office for further work.

When I work with clients using this, I usually work with their head of HR to guide them on writing these themselves. I sense to check them and give them feedback. If you're doing it in a workshop, you'll need one person to be in charge in pulling everything together and producing a single version of this for the business.

I include a session on these models in 21st Century Leadership, usually in Modules 4 or 5, depending on how much progress we've made on the Great Team Development module.

It's a session that involves you introducing the idea, the models and then having well-facilitated discussions about what's actually happening in your client's business. There will be questions about how to apply these models in your client's business. Here are my suggestions:

1 Use the behaviors cake model to start mapping your talent pipeline
2 Use the behaviors at each level in your job adverts, job descriptions, appraisals, performance, and career pathway documents
3 Use the behaviors to promote and also to let people go
4 Share the behaviors with your whole team so people know exactly what's expected of them at all levels and they know how to get on in your business
5 Combine these behaviors with a skill or technical matrix – include this in your people systems too.

Having the behaviors combined with the skills, and technical or professional qualifications needed in your client's business will give them a clear pathway to success in their business. It will give their leaders the ability to recognize and nurture talent and the business the opportunity to promote based on both cultural and commercial excellence.

This simple model is at the heart of building kick A** cultures in business! Who knew it would be in the form of a cake?

Figure 11.5 QR Code Talent and Succession.

Chapter 12

Employee Engagement

The People category features other models such as:

– Employee Engagement
  – Talent Acquisition and Retention, Succession Planning
  – Performance Management
  – Constructive Conversations
  – Great Team Development
  – Culture as a Foundation for Growth

Each of these has its own chapter.

Way back in 2006, I came across the notion of employee engagement. Gallup produced a questionnaire that helped employers understand whether their employees were engaged (I'll cover this in the next part of the chapter). This was the first time I'd heard the phrase, 'employee engagement' so I had to look into it further.

What I read was that research had shown engaged employees were more productive, took less time off work due to sickness, and tended to stick around longer. They also treated their customers and clients better. At the time I was running a recruitment business and thought this was something I'd like to explore for my team.

I sent the Gallup questionnaire to the team and got great feedback. We changed a couple of things to help improve communication and feedback for our teams, but essentially we had the right mix in the business of praise, feedback, meaningful work, autonomy, and friendships.

Since then, employee engagement has featured heavily in my coaching and consulting practice. I've encouraged every client I've ever worked with to consult with their employees at least once a year as to how things are going for them and then make sure they report on and communicate the findings. I also make sure they communicate any changes they've made based on the findings.

DOI: 10.4324/9781003540694-12

The Tricres model of employee engagement fits into the 21st Century Leadership Program in Module 5, alongside Performance Management.

As ever, Employee Engagement can also be used as a stand-alone workshop which could last a couple of hours, depending on the size of the group. It's also very useful in a one-to-one executive coaching scenario to help individual leaders understand how to work more closely with their own teams to increase engagement and productivity.

Here's a very simple wheel that gives you the top factors affecting employee engagement.

Engagement Drivers Wheel

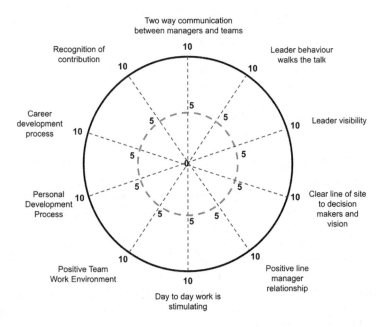

Figure 12.1 Employee Engagement Wheel.

Using the Engagement Drivers wheel is very straightforward. I introduce it to clients during 21st Century Leadership, Module 5 when we're discussing nurturing the individuals within your teams.

I simply ask them to first-rate how they think their teams would respond to each section on the wheel. Then I ask them to think about their levels of engagement and mark those on the wheel.

Even when I have board members on my 21st Century Leadership Program I ask them to complete this exercise. A couple of times they've realized that no one is looking after their development and they've formed a buddy/mentoring system or engaged me as a one-to-one coach to rectify that.

It's a useful tool for a discussion point too, let's look at it again in more detail.

Each person will give themselves a score out of ten as to how they feel about the statement, for example,

"There is two-way communication between managers and teams" – at Tricres, I feel that this is at a nine.

I also asked the room to mark how they think their team members would respond. In a leadership development context, this is a nice piece of self-reflection and should get the leaders thinking about how they are showing up everyday.

If an organization has an appraisal system, I'll suggest they incorporate this into that process and if they don't have a system, I'll suggest they use this wheel as the foundation for the system.

If I'm working with the board or head of HR, I'll how often they send out employee engagement questionnaires or staff surveys. Sometimes the answer comes back that this has never happened, in which case, I'll introduce the Gallup questions.

Employee Engagement Survey

	DISAGREE TOTALLY	DISAGREE	JUST ABOUT	AGREE	ABSOLUTELY AGREE
	1	2	3	4	5
1. Do you know what is expected of you at work?					
2. Do you have the materials and equipment you need to do your work right?					
3. At work, do you have the opportunity to do what you do best every day?					
4. In the last seven days, have you received recognition or praise for doing good work?					
5. Does your supervisor, or someone at work, seem to care about you as a person?					
6. Is there someone at work who encourages your development?					
7. At work, are you listened to?					
8. Do the vision and values of your company make you feel your job is important?					
9. Are your fellow employees committed to doing quality work?					
10. Do you have a good friend at work?					

Figure 12.2 The Gallup Questions.

There are several rules to sending out such a survey and your client absolutely must follow them, otherwise the whole exercise is a complete waste of time.

1 A communication must go out giving everyone a message about the up-and-coming employee engagement survey and reasons for sending it out. Such reasons might be to improve employee well-being, to measure the effectiveness of recent changes in culture, etc.
2 The communication with the survey goes out and all responses are received anonymously. There are several types of software you can use to do this – just Google employee engagement software and you'll find something suitable for your clients.
3 Responses are collated and the results are put into a graph with some explanatory text for each section. If the company has done this in previous years, some kind of comparison to past results is usually handy.
4 The results must be accompanied by a list of action points and comments from the leader of the business. These action points must be delegated to someone who will take full responsibility and accountability for ensuring they happen and communicated to the wider business.

I have seen businesses run such an exercise and it has failed miserably because they don't do point 4 properly, if at all. Advise your clients that unless they're going to make sure all four points happen, there is no point in surveying at all. It does more damage to employee engagement!

As a consultant and coach, you can offer to run this exercise so it's even further removed from managers and leaders, ensuring even more anonymity.

Figure 12.3 QR Code Employee Engagement.

Chapter 13

Performance Management

The People category features other models such as:

– Employee Engagement

  – Talent Acquisition and Retention, Succession Planning
  – Performance Management
  – Constructive Conversations
  – Great Team Development
  – Culture as a Foundation for Growth

Each of these has its own chapter.

When I first started doing workshops for my clients in 2010, I ran one called Performance Management. In true entrepreneurial style, I was asked by a very large global law firm if I could run such a workshop and immediately said 'yes, of course.' I then went away and did a ton of research on performance management so I could run such a workshop.

Faced with a room full of Partners, all of whom were probably paid about £1m a year I started the session with the Performance Focus Factors Wheel.

These are the key factors involved in performance management and performance improvement. However, I was with a bunch of smart lawyers and one of them thought he knew best.

He asked me a very loaded question, which went like this.

"Why aren't you teaching us about the feedback sandwich?"

If you're not familiar with the 'feedback sandwich', it goes like this.

You give feedback on performance by stating a positive first, then a negative, and then you finish with a positive. An example might be

"Sandra, you've been doing a great job on the Hormoxi Account, they love your work. I feel you need to step up your game on the Espresso Client though as their figures are low compared to last year. Your direct reports love what you do Sandra, so keep doing whatever you're doing there."

DOI: 10.4324/9781003540694-13

Performance Focus Factors

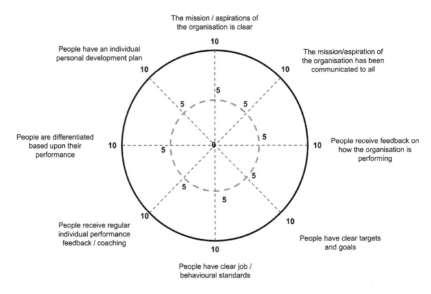

Figure 13.1 Performance Focus Factors Wheel.

The idea of the 'feedback sandwich' was that the less favorable feedback was sandwiched between two nice bits of feedback.

Now, my observations and my gut instincts told me that the feedback sandwich method of performance management just doesn't work. It doesn't work because we human beings are hard-wired to focus on the negative (it's a survival mechanism thing). Giving feedback to improve performance like this just gets people focusing on the negative and never hearing the positive stuff. It puts them in a downward spiral, which is not how you improve performance.

Mr Fancy Lawyer wanted an answer and sadly I reacted instead of responding!

I'm not proud of my reaction and have learned a great deal from it and have never done it since! I said, "Ahh, you mean the sh** sandwich method?" Swearing was my first mistake! "I won't be teaching you that today because it doesn't work and I make a point of training people in things that work."

You can hear the sass in my response, it was not my finest moment. Needless to say, he didn't come back after lunch and I got reprimanded by their Head of Learning and Development and was never used for workshops again. Lesson learned.

Interestingly, I've used the Performance Factors Wheel a million times since then and never experienced anything similar to that infamous event.

The lesson here for you all is twofold:

1 Always take a breath when responding, never react
2 Not everyone understands what drives performance. You'll always get leaders saying things like 'Well, they need to just get on and do it. I pay their salary,' etc. Your job as coach and consultant is to help people realize that performance and engagement are driven by culture, great leadership, and excellent communication.

Performance Focus Factors can be used in 21st Century Leadership in Module 4 or 5 depending on when you're delivering 'developing individuals' part of the programme and is best used when you combine it with Employee Engagement. It can also be used in a stand-alone workshop setting, again, I would advise you to combine it with Employee Engagement in this situation.

It can also be used in one-to-one executive or leadership coaching sessions to help the individual improve the performance of their teams.

Just like the Employee Engagement Wheel, I ask my groups to go through each statement and estimate what score their team would put in each section and then look at their levels of performance and mark their responses to the statements on the wheel.

The comparison between the two is often interesting and causes much discussion around performance.

Light bulb moments happen in the room as people identify where the weaknesses are in the people systems.

Let's look at a quick example from the wheel.

If you've done your work properly as a culture coach, the organization should have a clear mission and vision that has been communicated across the business. If this still isn't working, you may need to go back and revisit the purpose, vision and values and review how the business has communicated those.

If people don't have clear targets and goals, you can introduce the OKR system and suggest a workshop on that – if you're delivering 21st Century Leadership, that comes in Module 6 anyway.

If people aren't receiving regular feedback, you can suggest implementing an appraisal system or include the idea of feedback in the OKR system. Again this can be additional consulting work for you or included in 21st Century Leadership.

The clear behavior/job standards should be appearing in the people systems once you've done the purpose, vision and values workshop and helped the business embed the behaviors into their people systems and processes. If this isn't happening, you may need to revisit that too.

Each part of the wheel is an opportunity for you to measure progress in the business and to offer further support. It becomes clear to clients that what you've been talking about from day one directly impacts performance, productivity, and therefore success in their business.

I did tell you none of this was fluffy!

Figure 13.2 QR Code Performance Management.

Chapter 14

Fact Find

The Fact Find Process uses the following models:

- Economic Engine
  - Habits and Housekeeping
  - Players on the Pitch

Each of these has its own chapter.

My NLP training taught me that you cannot possibly solve a problem unless you know what you want the outcome to be and where you are right now.

The Fact Find is about you finding out where your client's business is at right now.

It uses three of the core models to unpack your client's People, Strategy, and Revenue systems. There are a multitude of ways to do this. Accountants use numbers, cash flow, budgets, and spreadsheets. Operations people use quality audits, process audits, and documentation. Different professionals will use different lenses through which to assess where their client's businesses are at.

At Tricres we're interested in the whole business as it relates to culture, people, strategy, and revenues. We want a holistic overview of these systems and want to uncover where the gaps are, so we can fill those gaps and build strong, positive, identifiable cultures.

The Fact Find is where you begin that journey.

During your meeting with the leaders of the business, one of the questions they usually ask, is 'How does the coaching and consulting work?'

I always begin by telling them that it starts with a Fact Find when they ask this question. If they don't ask this exact question, they will ask something like it if they want to work with you. It's a buying signal.

I then explain what a Fact Find is and how it works. I'm going to explain it to you, the way I would explain it to a client. That way you can just copy what I do!

DOI: 10.4324/9781003540694-14

I interview a selection of people from the business. Eight is a good number to interview, but I can speak to up to ten people. These people must be from the most recent hire to the longest-serving member of the team and include people at different levels with different skills in the business. I want a good, cross-section of the employee population to speak to.

I spend about twenty to forty-five minutes with each person and ask them a series of questions. These questions relate to the people, strategy, and revenue systems in the business.

I use the following models to frame the questions:

Players on the Pitch – this model helps me understand if you have the right people in the right roles doing the right things.

FUTURE GROWTH

This is the long term view.
It's how you'll make money in the
medium term, thinking 2 to 5 years.

Example

WHAT Choose the wording for the headings that suit your business best	WHO One person only
Culture	Raj
Partnerships and Joint Ventures	Puneet
Innovation and Design	?
Routes to Market	Jane
Product / Service Extensions	?
Talent Pipeline	?
Succession Planning	Suki

Figure 14.1 Players on the Pitch Future Growth.

I'll ask people if they know who is responsible and accountable for each area of the business. So using the Future Growth part of Players on the Pitch, I'll ask who is responsible and accountable for the Innovation and Design in the business. I'll ask this question for each section.

If someone doesn't know the answer, that's ok because that also gives me information about the business. I write down the name or names of the people in the boxes and collate a picture of who does what in the business.

NOTE: you'll likely get a whole list of names for most of the sections. What you want to achieve is one name for each section. It's only when a business has total clarity on the accountability and responsibility for each part of the business that it can truly move forward. Having one name means the buck stops with that person and it's more likely that things will progress in that area.

I repeat this with the other sections of Players on the Pitch

Example

WHAT *Choose the wording for the headings that suit your business best*	WHO *One person only*
Human Resources	Frank
IT	Saffron
Administration/Secretarial	Sanjay
Finance	Roger
Facilities (Office, Building, Cleaning)	Tracy
Legal and Compliance	Ramesh
Training (note, this is for regular, nuts & bolts-based training and not management or leadership development)	?

BUSINESS SUPPORT

This is the life blood of your business. Without this support, your business can't function.

Figure 14.2 Players on the Pitch Business Support.

Example

WHAT *Choose the wording for the headings that suit your business best*	WHO *One person only*
Marketing	Buzz
Sales	Amanda
Operations	Ritika
Client Services / Customer Care	Amanda
Talent Attractions, acquisition & retention	Charlie
Purchasing	?
Product or service delivery	?

ECONOMIC ENGINE

This is today's revenue. This is how you make money today and over the next 12-18 months.

Figure 14.3 Players on the Pitch Economic Engine.

NOTE: many small businesses have the owners doing lots of the Business Support stuff. These are areas where you can get quick wins by outsourcing this to freelancers or delegating to other team members.

This is the last section.

NOTE: if the owner of the business is good at sales, then they'll take accountability and responsibility for sales. If they're not, they need to find someone ASAP who is!

Be aware that some terminology in different businesses will be different. Go with the flow and simply amend some of the headings if this is the case.

The next set of questions focuses on the strategies a business has. This is where you use Habits and Housekeeping.

I'd like to cover something here that often comes up. Business owners who have built something from the ground up, often find it hard to let go of things. It's your job as a consultant and coach to help them understand they might be the blockage to the growth of their business.

If everything has to go through one person, it stops a business from being able to respond to changes quickly. It also means the business can lack innovation and diversity of thinking.

If you're finding it hard to coach the business owner into letting go of things, you might want to focus on finding something else they're more interested in doing. You also need to ensure the people they're delegating to are capable of taking on new responsibilities. This takes time and may require you to introduce 21st Century Leadership training.

Back to the Fact Find.

You'll recognize this as the Habits and Housekeeping matrix from Chapter 4.

So, the questions you would ask go like this:

Does the business understand the concept of people management?
Does the business have a written strategy/plan for people management?
Does the business action this plan/strategy?
Does the business have a way of reviewing this plan/strategy and changing it according to feedback?
Is the business using this plan/strategy to develop its 'secret sauce'?

The 'secret sauce' of a business is a unique way it does something. When you're working with a client, you'll recognize its secret sauce as you'll notice it does something in a way no other business in its sector or of its

	STAGE 1 Our business understands the idea	STAGE 2 Our business has a written plan for this	STAGE 3 Our business is actioning this strategy	STAGE 4 Our business has a feedback and review mechanism	STAGE 5 Our business knows and understands its secret sauce and is using it to grow
Project management					
Managing money					
Strategy					
Structure					
What we're worth					
Marketing					
Finding customers					
Sales					
Operations					
Relationships					
Culture					
Succession planning					
Future growth					
How we create value					
JV / Partnerships / Collaborations					

Figure 14.4 Habits and Housekeeping.

size does. For example, a hairdressing chain was so good at training its apprentices that it set up a training academy and now makes money out of offering that training to other hairdressers across the country.

You ask the questions I've outlined for each of the elements in the Habits and Housekeeping matrix. When I'm interviewing people for this, I place a tick, cross, or dash in the box and often write notes alongside the matrix. You can only put a tick in the box if the box preceding it has a tick. As soon as there's a cross or dash in the box, the rest of the boxes must have a cross.

The purpose of this table is to find out how the business is structuring itself for growth. If it has these strategies in place and someone is accountable and responsible for delivering on it then it's more likely progress will be made in an orderly and structured way. If there are no written strategies in place (they're often sitting inside the owner's head) then how will the business know what decisions to make and how will the leaders know which decisions they're allowed to make?

NOTE: when a business doesn't have these strategies in place (they won't have all of them at once, it takes time to build this range of strategies) it's often the case that the owner is the blockage to growth. Nothing is decided without his or her input and so things get stuck as there are only so many hours a day one person can work.

The final set of questions comes from the Economic Engine Model. Remember this from Chapter 3?

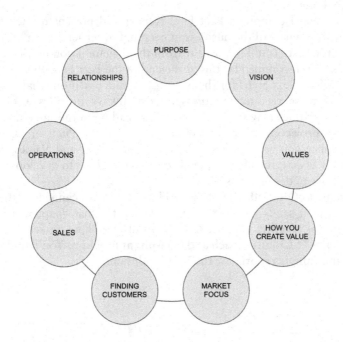

Figure 14.5 Economic Engine Model.

I use this to ask the following questions during the Fact Find:

1   Does the business have a clear written purpose that is shared?
2   Does the business have a clear written ten-year vision or mission that is shared?
3   Does the business have clear, written values that are embedded into its systems?
4   Does the business know whether it's a service or product-focused business?
5   Does the business know what its market positioning is i.e. Does it provide a mass market product or service at a low price or a niche product or service at a higher price? I find using the analogy of cars useful here i.e. Is the business more of a Rolls Royce or a small, second-hand car?
6   Does the business know where to find its clients?
7   How smoothly does the sales process work in the business?
8   What happens when a sale is made? Is the process a smooth one?
9   How does the business keep in touch with its customers even when they're not buying anything?

I take note of the answers and sit at my desk with a highlighter pen.

I then highlight the themes that keep appearing in all of the questions I've asked. I'm looking for gaps. I want to see what the business is doing and isn't doing.

From there, I compile a Fact Find Report and present it back to the board or the owners of the business in person. I never send it via email and hope for the best. You'll never hear from them again if you do that.

I make two recommendations at the end of the Fact Find Report which are the logical Next Steps for the business to take based on what I find.

One of these recommendations almost always includes a Purpose, Vision, and Values Day to get the business heading in the same direction. The other projects are usually either Players on the Pitch or Economic Engine. Once you've conducted the Purpose, Vision, and Values, follow the process as described in Chapter 1 to lead your client to develop an awesome culture in the business.

There is no QR Code for the Fact Find. If you've scanned a QR Code you'll notice it sends you to the single course for that chapter. If you've gone as far as entering your credit card details, you'll be offered the 'complete' Kick A** Culture Coach and Consultant Program. You'll find all the details and sample reports for the Fact Find there.

Chapter 15

Thinking Big; This Is for Your Mindset

Thinking Big includes some of the following models that you find references elsewhere in our Kick Ass Coach and Consultant Program:

- Thinking Creatively on Purpose

  - also in Strategic Thinking Made Easy
  - Great Team Development/Away Days
  - 21st Century Leadership

- PATH

  - Great Team Development/Away Days
  - 21st Century Leadership (if you have time, you can pop it into the team development modules)

- Keys to Achievable Outcomes

  - one to one coaching/or use a range of these questions with the boards you meet

- Vision Cards

  - I use these instead of sending complement slips or business cards, I slot them into my book and send them as gifts or hand them out at the end of 21st Century Leadership

In 2018 I was extremely annoyed and frustrated with myself and the world around me. I have a Master's Degree in Coaching, I was a qualified Licensed Trainer of NLP and I have over twenty years of business experience gained in a huge range of sectors.

No one wanted to employ me. No one wanted me to speak at their events and I didn't have many clients and the ones I did have were not of great quality.

I looked around for inspiration and I came across the work of Bob Proctor (he did the film The Secret). Now, he's a controversial figure who

DOI: 10.4324/9781003540694-15

has one or two models that he repeats over and over again. Love him or hate him (he died in 2022) his teachings helped me shift my self-image.

I wasn't even aware I had an issue with my self-image, but when I heard Bob explain why people just don't achieve their full potential it resonated with me.

When you see people less qualified, less able, less articulate, less talented, and less intelligent than you succeed, you have to ask yourself why. I did anyway. You might not.

Then I realized my self-image was wonky. It represented my rather scrappy, less experienced thirteen-year-old self. Yes, that's right, my self-image was stuck at age thirteen! I just didn't see myself or think of myself as an extraordinarily wealthy and phenomenally successful businesswoman.

Bob's teachings showed me how to do that.

I took what he taught me, added some more stuff I've picked up along the way and created Thinking Big (Really Big). I've tested it out on a few people and it really, really works.

If you follow the lessons and instructions to the letter, it will work for you too. Your self-image will shift and once that shifts, you are cooking with gas.

I absolutely would not have created Tricres, this book, our learning platform, our brand, or be building a global community of Kick Ass Culture Coaches and Consultants without having done this work.

I'd love to see where this program takes you and then your clients.

If you're interested in Bob's work, you can find it at The Proctor Gallagher Institute, here's the link https://www.proctorgallagherinstitute.com/

First of all, this is an ideal program for sales teams, recruiters, account managers, or a business that has huge targets to hit.

It works best with motivated people who are open minded to trying new ways of doing things.

You can also run it with micro businesses, I ran it during lockdowns over Zoom with a group of solo business owners and we had huge fun with it.

There are lots of downloads in the online program, so if you haven't accessed any of our online courses so far, then this is the one to get started with.

Just writing about it in a book doesn't do it justice.

The following information represents an outline of the four modules. There's a lot to take in, so get comfortable and maybe grab a coffee.

Module 1

This first part is about working out where you are now. If you don't have a clear idea about where you are now, then it's going to be difficult to work out where you want to go.

Get your group to complete Keys to Achievable Outcomes Questions. These are listed below:

1 What specifically do you want, remember to state this positively.
2 Where are you now?
3 What will you see, hear, and feel when you have your outcome?
4 How will you know when you have it – what's the evidence you'll be able to see, hear, or touch?
5 What will this outcome get for you or allow you to do?
6 Is it initiated and maintained by you?
7 When, how, where, and with whom do you want it?
8 What resources are needed?
9 For what purpose do you want it?
   What will you gain or lose if you have it?
   What will happen if you get it?
   What will happen if you don't get it?
   What won't happen if you don't get it?

People must keep these answers and bring them to Session 4.

If you're doing this for yourself or your clients, then brutal honesty is absolutely essential.

This first model explains why you get the results you get. If your thoughts are focusing on failure, lack of abundance, not getting great clients, and being stuck, then that is precisely what you'll experience in the real world.

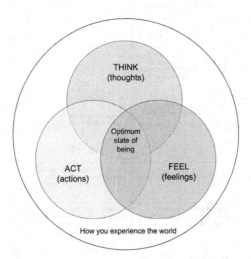

Change Your Thinking To Change Your Results

Figure 15.1 Thoughts, Feelings, and Outcomes Model.

Unlike Bob Proctor, I don't believe this is a magical secret. It's based on neuroscience. The reticular activation system in your brain focuses on the things you think about. If you're focusing on lack, failure, and disappointment then your RAS takes more notice of that stuff.

If you focus on abundance, success, and getting amazing high-paying clients, then you see more of that in the world and spot the opportunities.

If you don't believe me, then simply think about the last car you purchased. When you focused on the car you wanted, you suddenly started seeing more of that make and model of car on the road. Those cars didn't magically appear, they were always there. You just hadn't given your brain the instruction to notice them.

Your self-image was formed through school, parenting, your community, your religion, your early work experiences, your friends, etc. It often comes from other people's beliefs about you. By the time you're an adult, you are a different person than the one you were growing up. So much of the 'baggage' around who you think you are belongs in the past and was someone else's opinion anyway.

Where Are You Now?

CAUSE	THINGS YOU MIGHT SAY TO YOURSELF	EFFECT	THINGS YOU MIGHT SAY TO YOURSELF
• In control	• I choose my mood, my attitude and my emotions. • Sometimes I get down, but quickly change my thinking and move on	• No control or very little control	• I have no choice • The ____ (insert any word you like) makes me sad, angry, depresses me, upsets me E.g. Monday morning depresses me
• Empowered	• I make decisions about my work and my life • I make clear, conscious choices	• Disempowered	• It's my partners, parents, bosses, cats, dogs, cars, shoes, lunch etc fault.
• 100% responsible for my life	• I may not get things right every time, but I accept the responsibility for my outcomes • I know bad stuff happens in my life from time to time, but I choose my attitude and approach to it when it does and generally look for the positives	• Victim	• Nothing ever goes right • Everything goes wrong • People like me don't succeed • I can't... • Yes, but... • I know...
• Positive and generally happy	• I spend most of my time thinking about how things 'can be done' • I am generally in a good frame of mind	• Blame circumstance, people, the market, the economy etc	• It's the economy • It's the markets • It's the weather • It's the day of the week
• Choose own thoughts and beliefs	• Deciding what to read, watch and listen to	• Continue to hold the thoughts and beliefs that you've been given, even though they're not working for you	• Remain stuck
• Create your own self image	• Decide on your own strengths, level of risk taking, earning power, lifestyle etc	• Accept the self image you were given growing up, even though its not working for your	• Stay in your comfort zone

Figure 15.2 Cause and Effect.

It's time to start creating a new opinion of yourself, but before you do that, you need to do some unpacking of what this means in the real world.

You and your clients need to take full responsibility for your outcomes, take a look at our little matrix to help you understand what that means. If you're working with clients using this, go through this as a discussion point. You'll get some interesting questions and feedback.

The next matrix is about money. I ask my clients to complete this privately. This is because I don't want to know about their financial affairs and I'm not qualified to comment. If you're using this in a session with clients give them time and privacy to complete it. I often give it to them as homework.

Then they need to think about where they'd like to be financially. You too. Think about what you really want. Be creative, think big. This is your dream scenario.

You can ask your clients to complete the above matrix in the session if you wish. It can create a fun atmosphere and some good insights.

To create balance, it's important to focus on health, family, friends, and relationships in general. There is no point in being super rich and super miserable and lonely. By the way, everyone's definition of 'rich' or 'successful' is going to be different, so no judgment, please. Rich isn't necessarily about money, please make that clear to your clients.

Now you and your clients have gone through some of the basic 'unpacking' of where you are now. Make sure your descriptions of how you want

LET'S CONSIDER WHERE YOU'D LIKE TO BE (REALLY LIKE TO BE):

MONEY IN	ASSETS	SAVINGS/CASH	DEBTS/LIABILITIES
Money income £ (fill this out last, after you've worked out what you want)	Properties £ What do you want in property value?	£ What do you want in savings?	£ This might be mortgages you take out for properties, car loans or you may want ZERO debt. This depends on your risk appetite
Monthly Spends	Write out the value of the business or the annual income you want £	TYPES OF SAVINGS YOU WANT E.g. Bank, stocks and shares, pension	
Lifestyle			
Cars			
Homes			
Holidays			
Fun shopping			
Experience/Leisure			
Family/friends			
TOTAL MONTHLY SPEND			
TOTAL ANNUAL SPEND			

Figure 15.3 Where Do You Want to Be Financially?

		Score / 10	DESCRIPTION
HEALTH AND FITNESS	Describe your health and fitness today?		
	Where do you like it to be? Really like it to be.		
RELATIONSHIPS WITH A CLOSE LOVED ONE	Where are you today?		
	Where would you like to be?		
RELATIONSHIPS WITH FRIEND AND FAMILY	Where are you today?		
	Where would you like it to be?		
CAREERS/SALES BUSINESS	Where are you today?		
	Where would you like it to be? This is the big dream so spend time on this.		

Figure 15.4 Health, Relationships, Career Scoring.

to be are clear, rich, and focused. That means you add in lots of detail about sights, sounds, tastes, feelings, and even smells! The richer the description, the more easily your brain gets it.

Then you set the thermostat or the vision. When you do this the first time around, think of it as an initial draft. By the time you get to the end of the program, your vision or thermostat will be different.

This is your direction of travel. Without setting your direction of travel, how the heck do you know what decisions to make to get there? You don't. Setting a vision is crucial to making the right decisions today. It makes your life easier too. You can reject things that simply don't fit with your vision.

I say 'no' to things all the time because they just don't align with where I'm heading.

There's a huge section on this in the online program, way too much to put into the book. There are videos, audio, and other downloadable PDFs for you to use on yourself and with your clients.

If you only select one of our online programs to help you accelerate your coaching and consulting business, this is the one to select.

A note about setting a vision…some people don't do this at all and find themselves going through life very happily indeed. That's ok for your personal life and if it's worked for you so far, then stick with it. However, a business needs a clear direction of travel so if you're a business coach then you have a business and you need a direction of travel. This is likely to change as you mature, but without at least a sense of where you want to go, how on earth will you get there?

Module 2

When I deliver Module 2, I've already asked people to work on their financial, health, and relationship situations. I hope you've done the same. You need to know where you're starting from before you go anywhere.

So, until you've done those first exercises, don't even think about doing the next ones. The same goes for your clients.

Right, let's start building your self-image.

It's much easier to think about who you admire and why. You'll notice that I very rarely tackle anything in a straight line, I always take people on a mini-adventure to get to where they need to be. In my experience, the brain needs a bit of warming up before it gets to the answers that suit the human having a real-world experience.

Take a look at this matrix

List five people who you admire. They can be alive, dead, real, fictional, famous, in your family or friendship circle. Basically anyone you know of.

Name of person	Qualities you admire in them	How do they live?	What do they learn or study?	How do they present themselves to the world?

Figure 15.5 Who Do You Admire?

You might not like everything about them, but there will be certain qualities you admire. For example, I adore Elizabeth I, she was intelligent, well-read, determined, and knew how to manage herself in a hostile, male-dominated world. I do not admire her persecution of people who didn't agree with her.

It's perfectly possible to admire some aspects of a person while disliking some of their actions or behaviors.

List the qualities you admire about each person, then think about how they live. You might have to make this bit up, I don't know how Queen Elizabeth I lived, but I've read enough about her life and that period of history to give it a good guess.

You want to focus on how they conduct themselves, where they visit, how they speak, and what kind of company they keep.

Then you want to list the kinds of things each person studies, watches, or listens to. Queen Elizabeth, I read a great deal but didn't have access to YouTube, so that was an easy one for me.

Finally, you need to describe how each person presents themselves to the world. If you knew them personally, this is fairly straightforward, if you didn't, then there will be images, books, perhaps recordings, films, videos, etc. about them you can look up.

By the time you've finished, you've got quite a lot of information.

Your next task or your client's next task if you're running this as a workshop, is to highlight the common words or themes. What keeps popping up?

Highlight these themes and write them out.

Guess what? This is the self-image that you admire most and one which is already contained within you. You cannot identify with those attributes unless you recognize them in yourself. Whether you recognize them

Old self image	New Self Image
I'm tired, unfit and overweight	I am full of energy, fit and live well at a healthy weight for my body
I am unable to make more than £100k in fees a year	I am able to make £250k a year or more in fees.

Figure 15.6 Old and New Self-image.

consciously or unconsciously is irrelevant. You have now brought these attributes to your conscious awareness.

Using the next matrix (I love a matrix).

Write out your old self-image and your new self-image. Cross out your old self-image, or even better, write it on a separate piece of paper and then either set fire to it (safely) or shred it. You need to physically destroy the old self-image. If you're in a workshop setting, ask people to rip it up and put it in the bin.

Then write out your new self-image, using the information about the health you want, the things you learn, the money you have, the lifestyle you lead, the success you enjoy in business, etc. Keep it as you're going to need this later.

Make sure you state everything positively and as though you have it now. For example:

I read one book a month and I exercise three times a week. I love meeting new clients who have interesting projects to give me and who are happy to pay me well for my work. I really enjoy spending time with my family and friends, enjoying...etc. you get the idea.

Some of the very skeptical amongst you will be saying to yourself right now, 'This is a load of rubbish, what on earth is this woman on about?' That's my husband's voice!

Here's the science bit. Your brain cannot tell the difference between what you imagine in your head and what's happening in real life. You create the neural connections when you imagine something and your brain simply accepts that this is the reality of your life. This does not mean you live in a fantasy world that nothing bad ever happens or that you can sit on your sofa all day and do nothing. It means that by thinking great thoughts, you create great feelings and then you get great outcomes.

When life turns sour (and it will because that's just life), your attitude and approach are one of hope, optimism, and 'I'm the sort of person that can deal with this' when you make a decision to be that sort of person. You can still feel anger, hurt, upset, etc., but the difference is, that you recover faster, you make the decision to feel better about stuff and if something isn't working, you can change it.

This simple step of putting yourself in the driving seat of your brain is liberating. It takes practice and that's what I'm about to show you how to do.

Before we get to that though, I want you to make a commitment to yourself. The voice in your head is the one that you listen to most closely which is why the instructions you give yourself are the most important.

The act of physically writing something down is crucial. Researchers now know that physically writing things down helps embed them more effectively in your brain.

This last matrix is about making a commitment to yourself. I absolutely insist you write it out and then you sign and date it. If you're running this with clients, I want you to insist they do the same.

By the way, if you haven't noticed by now, the words I use with you in this book are the same as the words I use with my clients. You can do the same. Take my words and use them with your clients – make them your own, use your language, phrases, stories, etc.

Now, I want you to describe the kinds of clients and customers you want to be working with. If you've downloaded the Thinking Big (really big) PDF for Module 2 from the online program, you'll see there are loads of examples describing what you want for your business.

Make a commitment to yourself to make changes in the following areas of your life	COMMITMENT	ACTION AND COMPLETION DATE	SIGNED

Figure 15.7 Commitment to Myself.

You'll also notice, I tell a story about self-image that will bring this home to you. Essentially, it is about my friend who is a scientist and lawyer. She's very smart. Her husband is also a scientist, but not a lawyer. He's been very successful and she has seen some success, but not as much as he has. The self-image she has is one of lack of confidence, not good enough and unworthy of success. His self-image is the exact opposite. She had an Eureka moment one day when we were walking our dogs when she realized her husband was no better or worse than she was in their professional lives, he just thought about himself as really good at what he does.

Back to what you want for your business. Describe exactly what you want to be doing, how you want to work, who you want to work with, where you want to work, what you want to get paid and how often you want to work.

If you're doing this with clients, they can describe this for their business, their careers, or their own client base.

Keep this list. You'll need it later.

Understand this...you now have lots of ways to describe the life you want, the work you want, the business you want, the health and relationships you want and how much money you want.

Put all of these elements together and write out your script. It must begin like this....

"I am so happy and grateful now that...."

State everything in the present tense, for example, I had a friend who shared her daily mantra with me and it went like this:

1 I am amazing
2 I can do anything
3 Positivity is a choice
4 I celebrate my individuality
5 I am working toward success

I went along with points 1 to 4 and changed point 5 to

5 I am already a huge success

Can you hear, see, and feel the difference? If you're always working toward success you're never going to get there. If you're telling yourself you're already hugely successful, eventually you'll feel hugely successful.

If happiness is an inside job then so is success.

Most of you are already super successful. You wouldn't be considering being a coach or consultant if you weren't successful in at least one area of your life. My question is this, 'have you remembered to tell yourself you're already successful?'

Here's how you get better and better at what you do each day:
Five steps to mastering anything:

1 Know your outcome
2 Have excellent sensory acuity, notice what you see, hear, smell, taste, and feel
3 Focus on mind and body being the best they can. What you put into your body and mind is precisely what you'll experience in the real world
4 Behavioral flexibility, the person with the most behavioral flexibility in a system has the most power
5 Take massive action

Loads of people forget to do the last bit. When I say massive action, I mean a long series of baby steps. You cannot get from A to Z in one leap, you have to take all the steps in between, but take them you must.

Finally, do a bit every day. This book took 3 months to write because I did a little bit each week. I couldn't do a bit each day, but I knew I could do a bit each week. This is your razor's edge activity. If you're working with clients, it's the one extra call a day, the extra ten minutes with your team each day, it's the tiny activity that you add in and is always the difference that makes the difference.

The last thing for Module 2 is to decide to do it. Or make a decision not to do it. Either way, make a decision.

Most people fail because they don't decide to get going and keep going.

Module 3

Module 4 is a big one, if you have to put some of the content from Model 4 into Module 3 when you're working with clients, that's ok.

Module 3 is about tackling the objections people create when they're scared, nervous, unsure, etc. They know they want to change things and make a different life, business, etc., but it's a bit scary to get going. If you've been following this for yourself, you already know it takes work and effort.

Be gentle with your clients. They will need some tough love to get this work done. Or they may choose not to do it, just as you might choose not to do it. That's ok. It's not compulsory! There are other ways of achieving what you want, but I'm sharing the way I found the most effective to get my business and myself to where I want it to be.

Earl Nightingale defined success as 'the progressive realisation of a worthy ideal.' There are two words I want you and your clients to focus on.... 'progressive realization.'

Let's assume what you want to achieve for your own business is worthy and that your client's aims are worthy too. The rest of the equation is 'progressive realization.' It's that old chestnut of things taking time. You will make mistakes, you will learn from them and you will get it right or nearly right next time.

If you consistently have a go at something, tweak the bits that don't work so well and then have another go at it, you will gradually improve, be more successful and realize your dreams.

The first training courses I ever delivered were awful. The materials were terrible and I knew I could do better. My clients thought I was great though. They still got something out of the things I delivered to them. Only once did I think about giving up.

A rather arrogant medical academic spent an entire workshop putting me down and being rude. At the time, my ego and confidence were low and I nearly gave up. It was only later that I realized the problem was him. He was simply arrogant and rude.

Let's break your day down into sections. Many coaches and consultants fail to achieve what they want to achieve because they faff about (waste time, procrastinate, etc.).

Complete this table for yourself (honesty is key)

Where are you wasting time? Are you doing the things that get you to where you want to be or doing the things you want to be doing?

You're looking for a balance here. You have to allow for eight hours of sleeping time, at least four hours of 'downtime' with your friends and

TIME: FROM THE HOUR YOU WAKE UP TO THE HOUR YOU GO TO BED	ACTIVITY	DOES IT GET ME TO MY GOAL/VISION	IF IT DOESN'T - THIS IS WHAT I NEED TO DO INSTEAD
07:00 - 08:00	Wake up, eat breakfast	Yes	Keep doing it
07:00 - 07:20	Alarm goes off, press snooze 5 times	No	Get up when the alarm goes off- this gives you more

Figure 15.8 Daily Habits.

family and some 'you' time doing exercise, reading, painting, and staring into space.

It's about balance. You could work sixteen hours a day, but you'd have no friends, no family, and your health would suffer terribly. You'd probably end up rich, lonely, and sick.

Much better to work hard and work intensively during a reasonably set period. I choose to work Monday to Thursday from around 9/9:30 to around 4:30/5:30. On a Friday I try not to book any meetings and do things for myself like go swimming or meet friends or family for lunch, etc.

On Saturday and Sunday and don't check emails and I do the things I love doing.

There are times though when I need to do more work on my business and I'll add in a couple of hours on a Saturday or work throughout Friday. I then return to my preferred routine as quickly as I can.

I've come to this routine because it keeps me healthy, sane, and highly productive. You'll find a routine that does that for you. It will change as you go through the different seasons of your life. The main thing is that you're aware of what you need to function properly.

The other thing I do is book my holidays in my diary at the start of each year. When you're self-employed, it's really easy to leave things to the last minute and then a client wants to see you and you put your holiday off.

Your client will wait. Your holiday is really important. You cannot function well as a coach or consultant if you're tired and stressed. You'll burn out. You are your business so you need to look after yourself.

The same goes for your clients. Their teams need rest and recovery to remain engaged and productive. My husband never took a two-week holiday until he met me. He worked every Saturday morning until he met me. When he finally stopped working Saturday mornings and took proper time off, his business grew and he made more profit.

The two things are not a coincidence. He had more head space and more energy to think about his business. He got other people to do more of the 'doing' and he did more of the developing.

"But I can't". I heard some of you say. The question you need to ask is 'How can I?'

Whenever you hit a roadblock, there will be a million reasons why you think you can't do something. I want you to use this little technique to get over those roadblocks.

Write out all the reasons why you can't take regular holidays. These could be time, money, nowhere to go, etc.

Then cross those out.

In the next column write out all the ways you will go on holiday, for example.

"I will book one day off this week/month"

WHY I CAN'T	HOW I WILL
~~NEXT~~	
~~NEXT~~	
~~NEXT~~	
~~NEXT~~	
~~NEXT~~	
~~NEXT~~	

Figure 15.9 How I Will.

"I will spend that day in bed/reading/ meeting a friend/ going to a museum/gardening etc."

One day, small things that don't cost anything and bingo you have a holiday! If the blockage to what you want seems huge, start with small things you can do.

Don't even bother with things you can't change. Only focus on the things that are within your power to get done.

Finally, whatever you do in business, remember to give more value than the money you receive for your product or service.

Serve more people. The more people you serve, the more money you'll make.

Our podcast, this book, our learning platform, our social media posts, the coffees/Zoom calls I have, the courses, workshops I deliver, etc. are all about providing service to as many people as possible.

Start small. Do one thing at a time, get good at it, and then do the next bit. The podcast started back in 2019 because I love chatting to business owners, and this book started in 2024 because our learners said they needed a book, I still do the podcast and I'm writing this book. I didn't start both at the same time though.

You can only see the next thing once you've achieved the first thing. It's like climbing hills. You can't see the next hill until you've got to the top of the first hill. Stop trying to do everything all at once and just take one tiny step at a time.

Now, you're ready to put your entire vision together. Gather all your notes from Modules 1 to 3. Write out your vision in clear, rich, focused language, state it in the present tense, and write it so that someone coming along and reading it for the first time would understand it.

This might take a few pages and a few attempts to get it into the shape you want it.

Then read it out loud and record it.

Then play that recording back. How does that sound? Do you need to change anything? It does not need to be perfect; it will keep changing as you grow so go with what you've got right now.

Write out the entire script every day. Say it out loud every day. Play it back to yourself every day.

This feels stupid at first, but I promise you that if you keep going for three to six months, this will embed into your psyche and you will absolutely 100% believe it. Once you believe it, your energy changes, your language and your demeanor change.

You then become it.

Does this mean your bank account suddenly has millions of pounds in it? No.

Change Your Thinking To Change Your Results

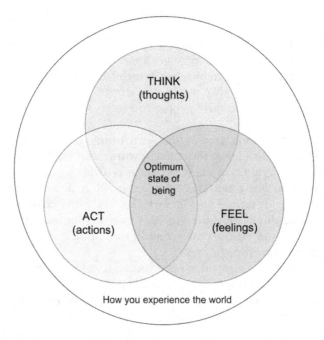

Figure 15.10 Thoughts, Feelings, and Outcomes.

Does it mean you suddenly get a zillion clients who pay you top dollar? No.

It means you begin to make different kinds of decisions and feel differently about yourself and your work. Remember the very first set of circles back in Module 1? Here's a reminder...

When you think differently, you feel different and your outcomes and actions are different. Change your thoughts, change your feelings, change your outcomes.

This process is about changing your outcomes. If what you were doing before wasn't working, then this entire exercise and program is just for you.

Humor me, you have nothing to lose and everything to gain by running this exercise. I did it and my family thought I was nuts. I didn't care. By the end of six months, I'd shortened my script and I felt like I could conquer the world. I still do and it's five years later. My business would not be where it is today or my life for that matter, without having done this exercise.

It's up to you.

Module 4

The last module is about bringing this to life. Let's get creative. Again, the Thinking Creatively on Purpose Exercise is on the online platform and it contains a much richer and more detailed version that I can provide here in the book.

Creativity is a process like any other. Jules Henri Pincare defined it as:

1 Preparation
2 Incubation
3 Illumination
4 Execution

Let's get you prepared.

Answer the following questions.

1 What are the five greatest achievements of your life?
   If you're working with clients, they'll usually come up with three or maybe four. I want you to encourage them to get to five. These can be small achievements like getting your first swimming badge or they can be huge like having kids or surviving a shark attack.

Then think about your purpose in life. What is it? What's your destiny? What were you put on this earth to do?

Then grab a load of colored pens, felt tips, and a blank piece of paper. Think about abstract art. You know, the paintings full of color, shade, dark, and light that don't look like anything in particular. The ones you look at and think 'My five year old could do that.'

Then draw the following emotions/concepts...

1 Happiness
2 Anger
3 Quality
4 Energy
5 Truth
6 Tranquility

If you found that hard, then that means you're using a part of your brain you don't normally engage with. If you found it easy, then good for you.

I've run this exercise with lawyers, accountants, tax professionals, risk analysts, managers, supervisors, CEO's, etc. They all love it. I encourage you to run this with your clients.

This exercise appears in away days and Great Team Development. I also use it in Strategic Thinking Made Easy, it also appears in 21st Century Leadership. It brings people together when you do it in a group setting.

Now, draw the following (still abstract)

1 The core issue in your life/business/career – pick one of these. You can do all of them but do one at a time
   Then draw, (still abstract)
2 What does your life/business/career, etc. look like when this issue has been solved? Again, pick just one at a time
   Now you can write!

Write down the change that needs to happen or as I like to say 'the difference that makes the difference.' What comes to mind? The change you need to make in order to get the result you want.

You're all loosened up and ready to put your creativity to a new task. Planning, creating a visual version of your big vision.

I get my clients to think about twelve months from now. You can think about twelve months from now too. I realize this might not be your timescale for your own big, giant vision, but there are milestones along the way and PATH represents one of those milestones.

PATH was created by a bunch of New York social workers who use it to help disadvantaged kids focus on what was in their control and what they wanted to achieve. Its full name is Planning Alternative Tomorrows with Hope.

The kids they worked with often could not read or write, so the exercise was done with pictures.

I want you to do the same because it's fun and it's in the spirit of the exercise. I do this each year and then pin the picture up behind my computer so I know where I'm heading. I did this year's PATH exercise three hours ago and it included a lot of books and podcasting!

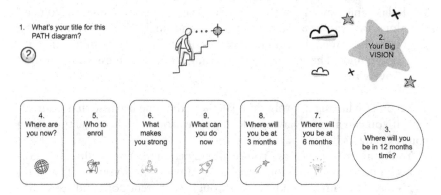

Figure 15.11 PATH Diagram.

1 Give your PATH diagram a title, you can draw OR write this
2 What's your big vision? Draw it, this is twelve months from today
3 Where will you be in twelve months?
4 Where are you now?
5 Who do you enroll to help you on your journey?
6 What makes you strong?
7 Where will you be in six months?
8 Where will you be in three months?
9 What can you do now?

Ask your cohort to review their Keys to Achievable Outcomes Questions they completed in Module 1. Have things changed? Do they need to tweak anything?

That's it.

Let's recap the twelve steps to Thinking Big (really big)

1 Have a desire to succeed
2 Create a vision and goals from that desire
3 Keep a strong self-image

4 Create new ways of thinking to create new feelings and actions through habit and repetition
5 Become very good at something you love doing
6 Think creatively
7 Take action, do something every day that gets you closer
8 Be persistent
9 Stay focused on your vision
10 Engage others to support you
11 If you're not getting the outcomes you want, change something
12 Relax, enjoy and trust the process. Please remember to enjoy yourself along the way because here's the last and final secret to Thinking Big (really big), the juice is in the journey. Do it happily, joyfully, and with good humor. There is no point in doing all of this unless you're having a lovely time.

You won't be having a lovely time 100% of the time because that's unrealistic. If you can aim for having a lovely time around 80% of the time, then you're doing well.

You're already a success. You're already enough. You're already a gorgeous human being. You don't need to do any of this if you don't want to.

It's merely an invitation to walk through a different door and see what's open to you.

Happy exploring.

Figure 15.12 QR Code for Thinking Big (Really Big).

Chapter 16

Twenty-First Century Leadership; a Leadership Development Program in Eight Modules

Twenty-first Century Leadership is about giving the leaders in the business you're working with the tools they need to lead themselves, lead the business, and lead their people and teams.

It includes all the other programs you've already learned about in the following order.

PLEASE NOTE: If your client needs you to run any of this in a different order because of what is happening in their business, please be flexible. Use your skills to give them what they need at the time they need it. You can always come back to something in a later session.

I deliver each module in a day for teams of eight and above. Teams up to eight, I'll deliver these in half a day.

- Modules 1 and 2 are about who you are as a leader and managing yourself
- Modules 3–5 are about leading teams, people, performance, talent, and succession
- Modules 6 is about leading the business
- Module 7 is about preparing for the presentation and returns to communication and messaging
- In Module 8, the participants deliver their presentation to you about their leadership journey

In 2017 I delivered my first purpose, vision, and values workshop to a client. It went well and the client loved the outputs.

They had (and still do) have a very good senior management team who went ahead and implemented the outcomes of that day into their business. They didn't need me to do it.

About six months later they came back to me asking if I could help them develop their leaders. They'd realized they needed a whole team of well-trained leaders to help them embed the values and behaviors across the business and help grow it sustainably.

DOI: 10.4324/9781003540694-16

This is when I realized this was true of most businesses. When the board wants to grow, they realize they need a very strong senior team to delegate to. They begin to understand they can no longer be 'operators' and have to move into the role of vision creators, strategists, and implementors.

The layers below the board usually consist of extremely skilled people in the specialism of that business. They very rarely have leadership skills, have very rarely received training in leadership, and often don't want the responsibility of leadership.

My client gave me a list of things they'd like their leaders to be able to do and get better at.

I used that list alongside additional skills to build 21st Century Leadership. Interestingly, in 2023, a large UK-based organization shared their research into developing leaders. Their program was almost identical to the one I'd created with my client!

During my Master's Degree in Coaching, I came across a fantastic journal entitled "The Leadership Pipeline" (Charan, Drotter, Noel 2001) I use some of the information around how people need to step up in different ways as they progress through an organization in my 21st Century Leadership Program.

Anyway, here's the Leadership Diamond which forms the basis of our 21st Century Leadership Model.

Figure 16.1 The Leadership Diamond.

Performance and Emotion

How might these emotions be observed in the workplace?

1 Euphoria Elation Joy
2 Expectant Peaceful Inspired
3 Passionate Excited Anticipating
4 Focused Clear Purposeful
5 Believing Confident Knowing
6 Hope Optimism Faith
7 Content Happy Calm

8 Bored Complacent Indifferent
9 Frustrated Irritated Impatient
10 Pessimistic Disappointed Sceptical
11 Discourage Disengaged Disheartened

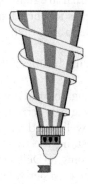

12 Worried Doubt Unsure
13 Overwhelmed Confused Stressed
14 Blaming Detached Dismissive
15 Judgemental Elitist Egotistical
16 Defensive Justifying Threatened
17 Resentful Bitter Aggrieved
18 Anger Jealousy Spite
19 Hateful Rage Revenge
20 Guilt Insecurity Regret
21 Fear Helplessness Anxiety
22 Depression Despair Shame

Figure 16.2 Helter Skelter Diagram.

All Modules, except Module 8, begin with a check-in using the Helter Skelter. We used this right at the start, but here's a reminder.

I've also attached a template agenda for **Module 1**. The pattern for each module is the same, except for Module 8.

Company ABC Leadership Today Session 1

Each session will start with a reminder of Company ABC's vision, values, and behaviors. As we go through each element of the program, the cultural aspect will be considered and explored to ensure thinking and actions are aligned. For this reason, there won't be a separate session on culture, it will run through the entire program like letters through a stick of rock.

Similarly, the commercial aspect of each element within the program will also be considered alongside culture, ensuring balance is maintained between commerce and culture.

Pre-work

Read the chapter on Leadership in "Good to Great" by Jim Collins, Watch Simon Sinek's TED Talk on How Great Leaders Inspire Action and read "The One Minute Manager" by Ken Blanchard.

Context: Growth

Level 3 Leadership – Managing Managers to Managing Functions

In an owner-managed or SME business, there are still elements of managing tasks that are required; however, this is reduced as the business grows.

Key areas for the Partners and SMT (Senior Management Team) leaders to consider about their role as they go through this program:

- Achieving business objectives through supervisors and team leaders

1 Learning about the wider business, beyond your own area of expertise. Learning new terminology and skills
2 Work well together as a senior team to get results
3 Understand the overall business strategy and be able to contribute to developing it. Delivering your part of that strategy within your function
4 Balance commercial and cultural aspects
5 Creative thinking, adaptability, behavioral flexibility, and strong communication skills are essential skills to develop at this level

09:30 Introductions

What are your expectations about today and the program?
What are your feelings about today and the program?
What do you want to get out of it – personally, for your team and the business?
What is great leadership?

10:15 Where are you now?
Go through each element so people understand it.

LEADERSHIP SELF -ASSESSMENT

	DO I	ADDITIONAL COMMENTS
People management and development	YES / NO	
Analysing data and getting into the detail	YES / NO	
Making clear, conscious decisions	YES / NO	
Creative thinking and problem solving	YES / NO	
Sellingand business development	YES / NO	
Planning and strategic thinking	YES / NO	
Project management and delivery	YES / NO	
Change- dealing with it and instigating it	YES / NO	
Team work with peers	YES / NO	
Presenting a clear vision and sense of direction for the team	YES / NO	
Public speaking and presentation skills	YES / NO	
Delegating effectively	YES / NO	
Managing myself and my time	YES / NO	
Where am I today on my leadership journey?	YES / NO	
What's my leadership style?	YES / NO	
Whatam I good at?	YES / NO	
What needs work?	YES / NO	

Figure 16.3 Leadership Self-assessment Matrix.

Use the model in your workbook to mark out of ten where you would put yourself on each of the elements shown.

This is the self-assessment matrix you should get your cohort to complete. They need to keep it as they'll refer to it at the end of the program.

Using the grid in the workbook describe where you are now in relation to your leadership journey. Some of the answers may only be one word, some may need more detail – if that's the case, then use your leadership program log book to make notes about where you are today.

Think about each of the questions along the top of the grid and relate them to the element of leadership listed down the side of the grid.

10:45 Now take a look at the model of leadership we'll be referring to throughout the program.

Give yourself a quick mark out of ten for each of the points on the triangle diagram. 1 = low ability and 10 = high ability in this area of leadership. This is only a very quick overview for you. The grid provides you with clearer details on the areas you need to improve.

11:15 Coffee break

11:30 Take a look at the image of the mountain. Discuss the role of a leader as the person with the longest-term view. Then discuss the role of the leader as the person who supports the whole business.

12:30 Lunch

THE LEADERSHIP DIAMOND

Figure 16.4 The Leadership Diamond.

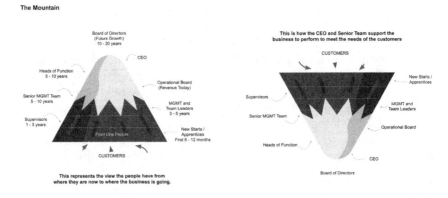

Figure 16.5 The Leadership View.

13:15 Video – remember Simon Sinek? Let's look at his views on leadership: How Great Leaders Inspire Action (YouTube 2009).

13:30 Discussion on the video and what it means for leadership.

How does this relate to you as a person?
Let's consider your personal values, attitudes, beliefs and behaviours Tree (this features in Great Team Development)

The Tree Diagram

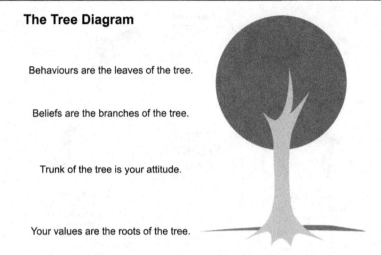

Behaviours are the leaves of the tree.

Beliefs are the branches of the tree.

Trunk of the tree is your attitude.

Your values are the roots of the tree.

Figure 16.6 The Tree Diagram.

What do you believe about yourself and your role?
What do you hold dear?
What's non-negotiable for you?

Having a clear understanding of your values etc will help shape your leadership style. It will also help understanding the people around you and how they relate to you.

14:00 Managing your mindset and your emotions.

Consistency and clarity are cornerstones of great leadership. Listening is a core skill.

Exercises in observational skills – peripheral vision, coin exercise.

Then the food you love/hate exercises with all senses, then just hearing, then just touch. This exercise is in Constructive Conversations.

15:00 Coffee

15:15 Action Learning set – how do you teach the rising starts how to lead?

16:15 Key learnings today.

Reflection exercise in your log books each week for one hour, using Gibb's reflective model – I'll be asking you at the start of each session to talk about extracts from your log books.

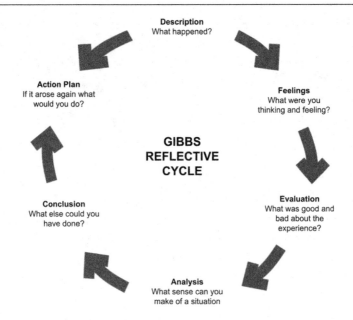

Figure 16.7 Gibb's Reflective Model.

So that's the first agenda for 21st Century Leadership. The rest of the agendas are in the learning platform.

The template for Action Learning, which features at the end of each session, looks like this.

Check In, how are we all doing?

Action Learning Model
Who you are? If the group don't know each other, make sure you allow people to introduce themselves.

Update from previous action learning (if applicable)

Bid

People in the room describe an issue they need the group to help with, keep it short and sweet

Selection
Each member of the group has two votes, they can vote for their own issue/bid if they wish. The group selects the issue/bid with the most votes. Allow approximately one hour per bid

Present the Bid
A Person describes the issue. The group listens ONLY at this stage. This takes about five minutes.

Feelings
Simply express feelings around the group on this issue. I encourage people to say one word, otherwise this stage can go on too long.

Option seeking
Good questioning. The person who owns the issue/bid sits back and listens to the group talking about the issue. They cannot say anything. I often get the person who owns the issue to move their chair back into a corner of the room or turn their back so they're not tempted to join in the conversation or give anything away through their body language.

They can write ideas down ready to present their thoughts and action plan to the rest of the group at the end.

You can repeat this process with the issue/bid with the next highest votes.

Again, if you want more details on how to deliver this to your group, please head over to the online platform.

Module 2

This is still about you as a leader and your leadership style.

I run the session with a full-blown run through of Constructive Conversations using an exercise around decision-making to get used to the six steps. See Chapter 9 for details on how to run a Constructive Conversations session.

Then we move on to delving a bit deeper into the mindset of the leaders. I use the exercise in Thinking Big which uses the following grid.

It's the one where the people in the room identify who they admire and the qualities they admire in them. As this is a leadership session, I ask everyone to focus on leadership qualities and leaders they admire.

I then use the following tool to help leaders understand where they might want to improve their leadership style. This is taken from Thinking

Name of person	Qualities you admire in them	How do they live?	What do they learn or study?	How do they present themselves to the world?

Figure 16.8 Who You Admire Matrix.

Old self image	New Self Image
I'm tired, unfit and overweight	I am full of energy, fit and live well at a healthy weight for my body
I am unable to make more than £100k in fees a year	I am able to make £250k a year or more in fees.

Figure 16.9 Old and New Self-image Matrix.

Big Module 2 and looks at their old self-image as a leader and the one they'd like to have.

As the facilitator of this session, I'm listening out for the gaps in people's leadership skills. I'm also listening out for their levels of self-awareness and ability to seek out answers for themselves.

Facilitating these sessions is a real art. You have to be able to listen and watch what's going on in the room, ask questions most of the time to elicit answers from the group and only from time to time give direction.

Participants will begin to form their ideas of how they want to show up as leaders through this process. Your job is to coach them to share the practical applications of testing out a new way of approaching a conversation or a problem in order to develop their leadership muscles.

I then use the Entrepreneurial Journey cycle to find out where they are now.

And have them notice what's coming next!

I encourage the leaders to write out their vision as a leader, stating it positively and in the present tense. I use the Vision Cards for this, these can be found in Thinking Big Module 4.

The Vision Cards have the following statement printed on them "I am so happy and grateful now that...." These are postcard size and have a blank space for people to write their vision statements on them.

Depending on time, you can run the "How You View the World" questionnaire or go straight to an Action Learning set. If you don't do the questionnaire here, do it in the next session as part of Leading Teams and Leading Others. I often find, I don't get to the questionnaire until Module 4 or 5 so don't panic!

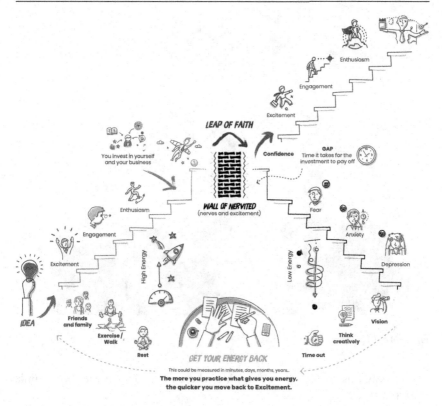

Figure 16.10 The Entrepreneurial Journey.

The "How You View the World" questionnaire is far too big and too detailed to fit into this book, so please head over to the platform for more information.

Module 3

We get into the people and teams bit here. I start with the usual check-in on what's happening in the business, and how people are and use the Helter Skelter to get people chatting.

I then introduce the idea of change. We all know it's the only thing we can guarantee in business, so I don't sugarcoat the need for leaders to navigate and embrace change. If they can't do this, they're definitely not going to thrive as a leader in the 21st Century.

The Change House model is a very widely known and used model. It's simple, easy to talk through and easy to grasp. I encourage the leaders in the room to share this with their teams.

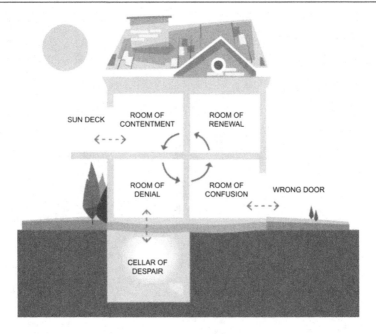

Figure 16.11 The Change House.

The way I use it is to start mapping where the people in the room think they are as:

A   A business as a whole
B   Individual team – this is their own team back at the office
C   Also, themselves as a group of senior leaders – they often don't see themselves as a cohesive team and part of your role is to get them working together to share best practices, solve problems, and collaborate across the business.

We then work through Tuckman's Team and Group Development Model – that's in Great Team Development so I'm not going repeat myself here!

I'll then get them working on the Creative Thinking Made Easy exercise and PATH, both of which are featured in Great Team Development and Thinking Big.

The idea of introducing these at this stage is to bring them together as a cohesive team and set objectives for their teams back at the office.

I also want them to start thinking differently about problem-solving and using these tools and techniques with their teams.

Module 4

This continues to focus on team development. I use the Team Diagnostic from Great Team Development and the Feedback Exercise featured there. Remember to use the model of the Tree before running this exercise, so everyone is clear about giving feedback based on behaviors.

As usual, I'll finish with an Action Learning set if there is time.

Module 5

In recent months, I've put Performance Management, Employee Engagement, and Talent Pipeline into Module 5. I found it easier to talk about this once we'd covered the Team Development part.

So, please visit those sections in this book and deliver them in your one- or half-day session with your cohort of leaders.

Remember to use the diagnostic tools both for the teams the leaders manage and for their development. Facilitating this can bring up some interesting points for the business that you need to feedback to the board or head of people.

Also remember to use the existing purpose, vision, and values of the business in the Talent and Succession part of this session. The organization you're delivering this for should have developed its matrix of desired behaviors based on the purpose vision and values work you did with them at the start of the process.

If they haven't, then please highlight this before session 5. It could well turn out to be an opportunity for more work for you!

You can help your leaders identify desired behaviors in the session if the business you're delivering this for has nothing available for you to work with.

It's at this point when leaders realize how important having the desired behaviors becomes. The penny drops! They finally understand how to measure and manage performance based on behaviors (culture) and skills (commercial). It's often the first time they've been able to articulate the difference and realize they can move seemingly high performers out of the business if they are a nightmare culturally.

This can be a game changer for businesses and leaders.

Module 6

I run through Strategic Thinking Made Easy for this module. Please refer to that chapter.

Module 7

During this Module, I prepare everyone for their presentation at the end. We spent the morning going over the matrix they completed in Module 1 which identified the areas of leadership they were good at.

I facilitate a session around where they've improved, and where still needs work and ask them to think about how far they've come. I also get them to look at the vision of leadership they wrote out in Module 1 and see whether they're close to achieving that.

It's a time to review and reflect, so I ask the group to complete Gibb's Reflective Model exercise again, focusing on the last eight modules. You'll find this in agenda I gave you in Module 1 of this chapter.

I ask the group to revisit the leadership styles sheet we saw in Module 1 and to review how they've grown to understand where and how to employ each style.

All this information, alongside any reflections they've put in their journals, is gathered together.

Then I talk about influence and persuasion and delivering a fantastic presentation. I use the materials my brother and co-founder, Nick Davies presents on our learning platform.

The next part of the session is focused on developing their communication skills. We use the form of the presentation they'll give in Module 8 as the goal. However, during the session I ask them to practice the skills in a 'mini-presentation' using a hobby or outside interest as a theme.

I get them started on the four mistakes people make when they're attempting to influence and persuade, these are:

1 Going too tough, that is, all guns blazing
2 Thinking influence and persuasion is a one-off event
3 Using way too much logic
4 Satisfying wants rather than needs

For the experienced coaches amongst you, you'll immediately recognize some of these errors in poor leadership!

We then discuss the need to build trust, and credibility and mix warmth with competence if you want to win your audience over.

The parallels between great leaders and the ability to develop these traits become obvious to the whole group.

Finally, we consider liveability, social proof, scarcity, reciprocity, authority, and consistency. These are the threads that run through all great influencers. While your cohort might not include 'scarcity' in their presentation about the leadership journey, it is worth noting that leaders should apply deadlines to their team so everyone knows what's expected of them and when.

There's a fantastic TedTalk (2009) by Bryan Stevenson that I show the group at this point. His balance of ethos, logos, and pathos is perfect. The perfect speech or presentation has the following balance of these things.

Ethos – theme, thread, lesson to be learned 10%.
Logos – logic, 25%
Pathos – emotion and feelings 65%

The more logical thinkers in the room suddenly realize why no one has been listening to them properly! They've been using way too much logic.

While we're discussing this, I ask them how they've been communicating with their teams. We often get to the point where they realize they should be telling stories, drawing pictures, showing people how they feel about something and adding humor. They begin to understand that showing data sets, spreadsheets, and endless bullet points just isn't getting the message across.

Then we move to the actual structure of their presentation. I show them the pneumonic SPICE.

Simplicity
Perceived self-interest
Incongruity
Confidence
Empathy

I then ask them to spend ten minutes preparing a mini-presentation (literally a maximum of five minutes and no slides are needed – they can use them if they wish, but it's not compulsory) which helps everyone in the room understand a passion, hobby, or interest they have outside of work.

It's fun, light-hearted, and prepares everyone for the presentation coming up in the next and final session.

I absolutely encourage everyone to be honest, and open and have fun with how they present their leadership journey.

I've seen leadership journeys described through the medium of cooking, art, cycling, fishing, mountain rescue, etc. It's been brilliant.

Module 8

Your cohort presents to you. Please invite the leaders of the business to this session if you can. Also, have a graduation lunch organized and remember to take the 21st Century Leadership Certificates with you so you can present them at the end.

People love this bit and even those who are terrified of presenting get into the spirit of things and enjoy themselves.

There's usually lots of laughter and sometimes some tears of joy or release of emotion. It's a wonderful end to a great leadership journey.

Remember to hand out the signed certificates (we have copies on our learning platform) and make everyone promise to be great leaders.

There is no QR Code for 21st Century Leadership. To access all the agendas, PowerPoint slides, and materials, you'll need to sign up for the full Kick A** Culture Coach and Consultant Program. This also gives you access to absolutely everything listed in this book, plus access to our community events and potentially joining us as a Tricres Coach (this is dependent on passing a case study).

The QR Code that is below.

Figure 16.12 QR Code for the Complete Kick A** Culture Coach Online Program.

Chapter 17

CRESCO Program; for Micro and Small Businesses

Part of the Tricres philosophy is to democratize access to high quality business coaching and consulting. We want the remote business owner on the side of a hill in Nepal to be able to use our content to grow their business.

That's why we train other coaches and consultants in our methodology.

That's also why I created the CRESCO Program. It stands for:

Culture
Roles and Responsibilities
Economic Engine
Strategy
Clear Leadership and Communication
Opportunities for Growth

It's a micro version of all the content I've shared with you in this book. It's delivered over half-day sessions once a month in small or large groups of people from lots of different businesses. There are six modules, so it takes six months to complete.

When I first stopped being a leadership and executive coach and went into business coaching, I realized there were hundreds of tiny businesses with big ambitions who needed my help (or any help).

While government-backed programs are good and scale-up programs are good, they don't cater to those businesses that aren't in the tech or biotech or edtech or any tech sector. They're not the sexy businesses. None of them are ever going to raise investment beyond close family and friends and no equity house is ever going to give them the time of day.

These businesses are actually the backbone of every single economy on the planet. They're the mom-and-pop stores if you're in the USA, they're the small coffee chains, the small manufacturers, the craft person, the tea entrepreneur, and the professional services businesses that want to build something suitable for their owners, the small number of staff they employ, and their clients and customers.

DOI: 10.4324/9781003540694-17

Sometimes, these businesses go large. Quite often, they build very slowly and create wealth for their owners, their immediate families, and their communities.

CRESCO is built for these people. They can't afford a consultant or coach one-to-one, but they can afford a few hundred dollars or pounds a month to join a group of like-minded business owners who want a forum to share their issues and a structure to help them navigate their growth.

I first ran this with a pre-revenue start-up, someone who'd been made redundant and was considering her options, a coffee shop entrepreneur, a stage lighting entrepreneur who'd just become an employee-owned business, a student, and a recruiter. It was an eclectic bunch of people and so the learning was excellent.

I hired a room in my local bank (they do the room hire for free for customers) and set the dates in advance. I also set up the repeat invoicing on Xero (Quickbooks is a similar package used in the USA) for six months so I have revenue coming in each month.

It worked a treat for me and the learners.

All Modules begin with a check-in using the Helter Skelter (see Figure 17.1 on the next page). We used this right at the start and in 21st Century Leadership, but here's a reminder.

Module 1

Create Your Culture and Mindset

Each session has one of the Tricres core frameworks and something taken from Thinking Big (really big). This is because the biggest issue I found with micro businesses is mindset and basic business structures.

I would also encourage you and your attendees to read The E-Myth Revisited by Michael Gerber. I recommend this book to all micro-businesses, it's excellent.

During this first session, you'll run a shorter version of Purpose, Vision, and Values as described in Chapter 1. It will consist of the morning session of that workshop and each participant will be answering the questions based on their own business.

Then you'll take your group through the Keys to Achievable Outcomes Questions as seen in Thinking Big Module 1, here's a reminder.

1 What specifically do you want, remember to state this positively.
2 Where are you now?
3 What will you see, hear, and feel when you have your outcome?
4 How will you know when you have it – what's the evidence you'll be able to see, hear, or touch?
5 What will this outcome get for you or allow you to do?

Performance and Emotion

How might these emotions be observed in the workplace?

1 Euphoria Elation Joy
2 Expectant Peaceful Inspired
3 Passionate Excited Anticipating
4 Focused Clear Purposeful
5 Believing Confident Knowing
6 Hope Optimism Faith
7 Content Happy Calm

8 Bored Complacent Indifferent
9 Frustrated Irritated Impatient
10 Pessimistic Disappointed Sceptical
11 Discourage Disengaged Disheartened

12 Worried Doubt Unsure
13 Overwhelmed Confused Stressed
14 Blaming Detached Dismissive
15 Judgemental Elitist Egotistical
16 Defensive Justifying Threatened
17 Resentful Bitter Aggrieved
18 Anger Jealousy Spite
19 Hateful Rage Revenge
20 Guilt Insecurity Regret
21 Fear Helplessness Anxiety
22 Depression Despair Shame

Figure 17.1 OKR Grid

6 Is it initiated and maintained by you?
7 When, how, where, and with whom do you want it?
8 What resources are needed?
9 For what purpose do you want it?
10 What will you gain or lose if you have it?
11 What will happen if you get it?
12 What will happen if you don't get it?
13 What won't happen if you don't get it?

People must keep these answers and bring them to session 6.

Take a break and then complete the Self-Image exercise from Module 2 in Thinking Big.

Set tasks between sessions, these will be based on what happened during the session. A good task might be to complete a vision card or write out their new self-image. Some tasks might be more business-related and require people to take action.

Your role is to act as facilitator, trainer, and group coach for this cohort so you need to use all your skills to respond to the needs of the group. Each time you deliver this, it will run slightly differently because you have different people with different needs in the group.

If you've been following this book closely, you'll understand that having behavioral flexibility is absolutely key.

Module 2

You'll run the **Players on the Pitch** exercise here. Take your cohort through each of the roles and responsibilities in Players on the Pitch. Use the grids we provided in that chapter to get each of your participants to work out who does what in their business.

As they are micro businesses, their names will appear in almost all of the sections!

As a facilitator, you need to help them work out what they can outsource. There are so many options these days that they don't need to struggle on their own.

This is a great time to help them understand how to delegate and the difference between delegating a task and a responsibility. It's also a good time to help them stop micro managing and think about where they need to put their energies.

After the coffee break, move on to where your participants are in terms of their life, health, relationships, money, etc. Use the financial, health, and relationship matrix from Thinking Big Module 1 for this part.

Make sure your audience understands they can create the business to suit their lifestyle. No one has to build a multi-million dollar business, it's not compulsory. People can build smaller businesses and have a great life. It's so important business owners build a business to suit who they are and their current season of life.

Again, review tasks from the last session and set more tasks for the next session.

Module 3

Economic Engine

Take your cohort through the nine circles of the Economic Engine and find out how their business is doing for each one. The answers in your group will dictate where you focus this session.

Many micro businesses have never considered using a CRM (Customer Relationship Management), and they may not have systems to keep in touch with customers or send out offers.

This session can get quite detailed. Make sure you have the knowledge and tools to make recommendations. We recommend HubSpot to get people started on a CRM system and either Mailchimp or ActiveCampaign for email systems.

There are industry-specific systems and I'd encourage your cohort to look into those if they work in specialized sectors.

The important thing is they know and understand what a sales cycle is and how to make sure it runs smoothly.

The element from Thinking Big in the session is the Razor's Edge activity. What small additional task can they do each day to get one step closer to their goal?

Make sure your cohort writes down what they're doing to do, so it gets done. This is also a good time to get them to write down the commitment they are making to themselves about their own health and well being. Again, this comes from Module 3 in Thinking Big.

Review tasks and set new tasks.

Module 4

Strategy and strategic thinking. I had not created Strategic Thinking Made Easy or OKRs Made Easy when I ran my first CRESCO program. Your life is much easier now I have!

I would show people the Horizon Model just to illustrate the "golden thread" between the purpose and the individual OKRs and checkpoints.

The "golden thread" is the term I picked up from a client. They use it to help everyone in the organization understand how their individual strategies need to align with the organization's overall strategy.

Simply run Strategic Thinking Made Easy and OKRs Made Easy for this session.

Add in the Vision cards at the end so people can write out their desired vision.

Remember to check in on tasks and set new ones.

Module 5

Clear Communication and Leadership

You'll run through the whole of Constructive Conversations for this session. Combine it with the leadership diamond I showed you in 21st Century Leadership.

I'd ask your cohort whether they want to work on themselves as leaders or work to develop their team and individual team member leadership skills.

You'll only have time to cover one of those during the session, so it's a good idea to see what your cohort needs. Depending on what they say will dictate whether you run through the Great Team Development diagnostic, Change House, and Truckman's models or whether you give them the questions around their own leadership styles and discuss those in more detail.

Either way, you'll have enough materials in 21st Century Leadership to blend what they need for this session.

Module 6

Opportunities for Growth

This is where you help your cohort set their path to success.

Ask them to complete the Growth Accelerator matrix for their own business so they can see where the gaps are. They also need to understand that adding value by increasing the multiple of their business will make it stronger and more likely to succeed.

Complete the session with Thinking Creatively on Purpose and PATH, both can be found in Module 4 in Thinking Big.

Complete any last reviews of tasks and check in to see how far people have come since starting the program.

You might want to capture some short video testimonials at this point for your own social media channels!

Get referrals and set up a waitlist for your next CRESCO cohort.

There is no QR Code for CRESCO. To access all the agendas, PowerPoint slides, and materials, you'll need to sign up for the full Awesome Culture Coach and Consultant Program. This also gives you access to absolutely everything listed in this book, plus access to our community events and potentially joining us as a Tricres Coach (this is dependent on passing a case study).

The QR Code that is below.

Figure 17.2 QR Code for the Complete Kick A** Culture Coach Online Program.

Acknowledgments

My wholehearted thanks go to my teachers, every single one of them has taught me something you'll find in this book.

From my favorite primary school teacher, Mrs Critchlow to Dr Richard Bandler, John and Kathleen La Valle, and the Society of NLP Trainers. They've taught me to show up consistently, to be curious, to read everything and anything, and to practice.

None of this work was easy. It took hours and hours of time and thousands of pounds of investment. It's shared with you in the spirit in which it was taught to me: wholehearted enthusiasm and honesty. Please pass it on in the same way.

With love

Rebecca

Index

Note: **Bold** page numbers refer to tables and *italic* page numbers refer to figures.

Printed in the United States
by Baker & Taylor Publisher Services

Printed in the United States
by Baker & Taylor Publisher Services